GETTING AHEAD: IN THE ERA OF AI

REVAMP YOUR LIFE WITH A TECH-ENHANCEMENT APPROACH

N J SHARMA

Made with ❤ on the Notion Press Platform
www.notionpress.com

Quoting Rabindranath Tagore "The one who plants trees, knowing that he will never sit in their shade, has at least started to understand the meaning of life."

I dedicate this book to all the great minds throughout humanity's existence, who have all contributed to the technology and advancements we have today. Without them, our society wouldn't be what it is today.

While some of them are known, majority remain nameless or forgotten, just like grains of sand that get carried away by the wind. It is praiseworthy to possess the kind of dedication that allows you to continue working, knowing that your hard-work will be of use long after you have departed from this world. This selfless act of contributing to the betterment of humanity is truly one of the noblest sacrifice a person can undertake.

And that is what Rabindranath Tagore was implying in the quote, at least that is how I understood it :)

Contents

Preface

We're in the era of AI, a technology even more invasive than the internet. You don't have to be good at tech to get used to it. Just have a basic understanding of it, like knowing the basic rules of a sport; being a professional player isn't necessary to understand the game.
If you've seen sci-fi movies or read science fiction books, most of them have a similar theme. Set in a dystopian future; the society is characterized by advanced technology, a scarcity of resources, a fragile government, and an extreme socioeconomic divide.

We are still a long way from those times, hopefully, but with the recent spread of AI, we can see it beginning to take hold. It's being slowly implemented into every little aspect of our personal and professional life, directly or indirectly. In the future, it's only going to become even more prevalent.

The smarter decision is to learn about technology now, before it gets too big and complex for many of us to adapt. So yes, people who adopt and get proficient with the latest technologies, will inevitably be the ones Getting Ahead.

Introduction: A World Full Of Possibilities

"AI is akin to free-flowing water, steering in whichever direction we guide it" - me

The media is buzzing with discussions about Artificial Intelligence and it's future, making it impossible to ignore. A technological shift is happening, and we're right in the middle of it. You might be wondering, what exactly is a technological shift? Well, in simple terms, it's when we are suddenly bombarded with 'AI' products by every company, even if many of them miss the point of what being smart is (*with paid subscriptions, of course*). And don't forget the keyword "AI" being thrown around at you, at every possible instance; in all forms of social & news media, that we see or hear everyday.

Artificial Intelligence has become so prevalent that it is now being integrated into common household items like refrigerators, air-conditioners, toothbrushes, and even weighing machines, making these boring machines 'smart'. Thanks to the advancements in science and mathematics, traditional products have undergone a remarkable evolution, with features and hardware that were supposedly deemed impossible to implement just 20 years ago.

To give you a sense of how convenient technology can be, Imagine this: I had a busy day at work and I couldn't wait to go back home, I turned on the water heater with my phone so I can hop into the shower as soon as I get back. The moment I reached my house, I instructed my voice assistant to dim the lights and play my go-to playlist through the smart home speakers, setting the perfect ambiance for the evening. After a relaxing shower I check with my voice assistant for any pending reminders before settling onto the couch to stream some relaxing wildlife documentary, while I treat myself to dinner. Then I tell the voice-assistant to set an alarm and give me a heads-up about tomorrow's meeting at 7AM.

For morning workouts, my smart-watch is the perfect trainer as it tracks my health metrics and gives me suggestions on how to be more effective with my workout routine. Following breakfast, I double-check my usual commute route to be sure that no unexpected closures or delays will cause me to be late for my meeting. I hop in my car, turn on some relaxing beats, and head to work. When I reach my office, I tap my office access tag at the entry and quickly sync up today's schedule with the cloud.

This is just one example to give you an idea of how different technologies are already present in our lives, but the truth is, there's technology involved in pretty much everything we do. It has become an integral part of our lives, regardless of our individual routines, and as more products become digital or smart, it will become unavoidable. The pace at which change is taking place has sped up so much that our interactions with objects, individuals, society, and our environment are now barely recognizable from what they were a mere ten years ago.

Thanks to modern chips, AI is finally picking up speed.

The value of having a plethora of chips extends beyond phones. These chips are crucial for IoT devices, enabling effortless transition of data and access to a multitude of smart-products that require diverse technologies to function cohesively. The need for multiple 'AI' chips in every individual smart-device is tackled by spreading them across your phone and smart-watch, which facilitates convenient access and monitoring of each AI-enabled device. Therefore, devices can communicate efficiently via an active wireless/wired network.

Think of your phone as a remote that can control the multiple smart devices that you own, with each app serving as the button to access them. Having so many devices connected manually would be a headache for even the most patient people, but having AI manage all the annoying and complicated tasks makes it easier for the majority of people to use these devices as part of their everyday lives without being constantly hindered in their activities. Seamless connectivity and transition from one device to another is something many people don't realize the importance of, but makes for a huge difference. One of the major reasons for Apple's success is the focus on their eco-system with different Apple devices and software.

A revolutionary technology is here, and it's going to spread at unprecedented rates.

Artificial Intelligence has made huge waves and trying to keep up with rapid changes can be challenging, leading to feelings of being left out or being overwhelmed. When we understand why and how change happens, we are better equipped to adjust and evolve with time.

And it's not just the layman who falls prey to this trap. If we go back to 90's; news media, experts, and influential individuals across industries, predicted Internet's downfall within a decade, erroneously labeled it as a mere fad, not because of their outright denial but their inability to grasp the unparalleled qualities and possibilities that could be created with the internet. The validation of the naysayers and doubters of the Internet was further solidified when the Dot-com bubble, which saw the US market skyrocket by over 800% in the 90s, eventually burst, causing the market to plummet by 740% until 2001.

However, a certain proportion of society held onto the idea that the Internet's potential was not in its present state, but in a future where technology and science would be more advanced, and thus, persevered in their endeavors. Motivated by their unwavering determination to push boundaries, many investors, engineers, scientists and business leaders went to great lengths to seek out and hire the most skilled professionals from around the globe, financed R&D and experimental technologies to make their vision for the future of technology a reality. The competition was so cutthroat that new companies were popping up left and right, taking market shares away from traditional and established organizations across industries.

Thanks to its early adoption and the implementation of business-friendly policies, the United States emerged as the biggest winner of this dot-com transition, establishing itself as a global hub for both technology and business. The presence of numerous major tech companies and prominent individuals in the US, today, is undeniable.

And after 2 decades of consistent competition, we finally saw this race settling down. The market distribution of tech companies was rather predictable between 2013 and 2018, however, this has once again shifted after the pandemic. The development and investment of AI-based technologies has increased rapidly in response to the pandemic; for established brands, the investments into AI R&D soared from $49 billion in

2019 to $93 billion in 2021. According to the tortoise global AI index, global AI investments more than doubled from $36 billion in 2020 to $77.5 billion in 2021.

On the other hand, global semi-conductor industry plans to invest over $500 billion in their quest to expand around the world because the demand for chips is going to skyrocket with smart-products seeping through in almost every industry. With governments and businesses focusing so much on AI and semi-conductors, it's no wonder this drastic shift in the economy will affect not just organizations but everyone. The availability of job positions within companies is in a state of flux, reflecting the changing market trend.

How history embraced technological shifts.

When industrialization happened, people feared machines will replace humans. During the global internet boom of 1990-2001, concerns arose about the potential loss of jobs for people. However, instead of jobs becoming scarcer, it was the roles and positions that transformed, as well as new positions being created for the various skills needed for operating the latest technologies. In fact, the number of positions available kept on increasing as industries and organizations kept growing between 2005-2018. Although many traditional companies closed down, the emergence of new companies and job opportunities signaled a stable growth in the market.

We can say the same for today's market. The pandemic resulted in record layoffs as companies sought ways to minimize losses and automate traditional jobs. However, I am certain that AI will generate more employment opportunities than ever before, albeit with a unique set of new and specialized skill requirement. With companies gradually shifting strategies and business models to incorporate AI in different ways, we can see the current period of job uncertainty as a correction. Once the dust settles, market will be infused with the smell of freshly brewed coffee and the sounds of conversations as companies resume hiring for new roles and competencies, signaling a return to stability and growth.

Although, the success of AI depends on a variety of factors, despite its status as a groundbreaking technology; cultural habits, hardware/software progression, profitability, social trends, global policies, and infrastructure development, all affect it's implementation. AI operates in tandem with other technologies, augmenting the need for industry-specific expertise and skilled workforce. Thus, conventional jobs are dwindling and will eventually become obsolete.

Just as with previous technological and industrial advancements, social trends have progressed in a similar manner over the last few centuries. The transition from one prevailing industry to another has had a profound effect on social habits and trends throughout human history.

In the 18th and 19th century there were greater disparities in fashion, habits, jobs, forms of entertainment, and family dynamics between the upper, middle, and lower classes. The correlation between these factors and the professional status of the men and their social circle was direct. Although not as common as before, professional life still has a considerable impact on an individual or family's social life and hobbies.

The evolution of media has taken us from newspapers, to radio (FM/AM), then to television, and finally to computers and smartphones. In the 1800s, newspapers and magazines provided a platform for people to express their opinions and inquiries, while radio allowed for real-time discussions that were accessible to everyone. Live interviews, social gatherings, entertainment media, and political events became more accessible to people regardless of their economic status with widespread consumerism.

The social impact of modern technology.

Social media platforms further broke down barriers and gave people the opportunity to interact with anyone, anywhere in the world. The use of technology has effectively minimized the divide among different cultures, ethnicities and nationalities, even enabling people to converse in different languages using a live translator. With my phone's translator, I've talked to people from over 15 countries. 30 years ago, this would've been like a dream!

The global impact of social media is so immense that virtually every nation has attempted to establish its own platform or entice social media entrepreneurs to tailor the platforms to their country's needs. It is not a coincidence that there has been a sudden surge in AI either. The rise of the Internet, social media, and smart devices over the last two decades has been driven by the desire to attract as many people as possible and gather as much data as possible. With the billions of users' worth of data now collected globally, AI-based software is being fueled by this very data.

What's remarkable is that social media, which was created for a very different reason, has emerged as the most significant source of data and influence over social and political trends globally. Only after years of observation did companies recognize the enormity and potency of social media. It proved to be far more complex and far-reaching than governments initially anticipated, and they are only just beginning to understand its implications, especially since the pandemic made it clear just how much influence it has over people's opinions.

It's only going to grow more now.

Social media platforms currently house a massive 4.9 billion users across the globe, and this number is expected to rise significantly over the next five years, especially in developing regions, like Africa and South Asia, where internet accessibility is expanding and population density is high. I expect the impact of Internet on humanity to be profound, second only to that of electricity. Internet has provided the means for entire countries, as well as businesses, to undergo transformation.

Since the surge in AI based products, many newer industries and startups are thriving while established brands are facing tougher competition. To name some newer industries of the many: Robotics, Bio-technology, Food technology, Wearables, Virtualization, AR/VR, Human Augmentation, and FinTech. As industries try to adapt to the changing market, the skill requirement will change as well and it is changing at an unprecedented rate.

The next 20 years could see AI outpace the Internet in terms of impact. We could make AI that is self-sufficient and rules over humanity, just like those evil robots in sci-fi movies, or we could make it into something that helps humanity and earth to sustain in the long term while also improving the quality of life for everyone.

Imagine we are in 2050. You go out and there are self-driving cars on the road, some cars hovering just above the ground, drones flying in the sky. Holographic images and videos playing in the sky, just like those in blade runner. Everyone would have their own AR wearable that displays a screen right in front of their eyes as they walk, without having to stop and look. And that's barely scratching the surface, technology will become even more widespread in the future, surpassing barriers that it has today.

So, let's start our self-improvement journey.

The first chapter will give a succinct overview of the functioning of AI and the technologies connected to it. The rest of the book will delve into the profound effects of AI on our professional endeavors, personal relationships, and social interactions. In addition to covering those topics, there will be helpful tips on how to adapt and adjust to these changes. So make sure you don't skip the important parts.

CHAPTER ONE

Dissecting AI and Robotics: An Overview

AI serves as an umbrella term, catering to mass marketability and advertisement, but behind it lies a multitude of interconnected technologies that enable the functionality we associate with smart and AI features. The goal of this chapter is to deep-dive into the functioning of different technologies that enable and enhance AI. These concepts are important and hold values that have practical implications beyond just the book and into our real-world experiences and interactions. (more onto the co-relation of technology and our brain later).

AI has been in existence since 1940's, although the term AI was coined in 1956, and has been in the works ever since. It was only until very recently, that we are seeing different forms of AI being implemented across a variety of devices. There are a lot of different technologies that empower the buzzword 'AI', and some of them have seen major advancements in recent years, thanks to modern hardware and software improvements.

For visualization, here is an image with some of the major concepts that make-up the term AI:

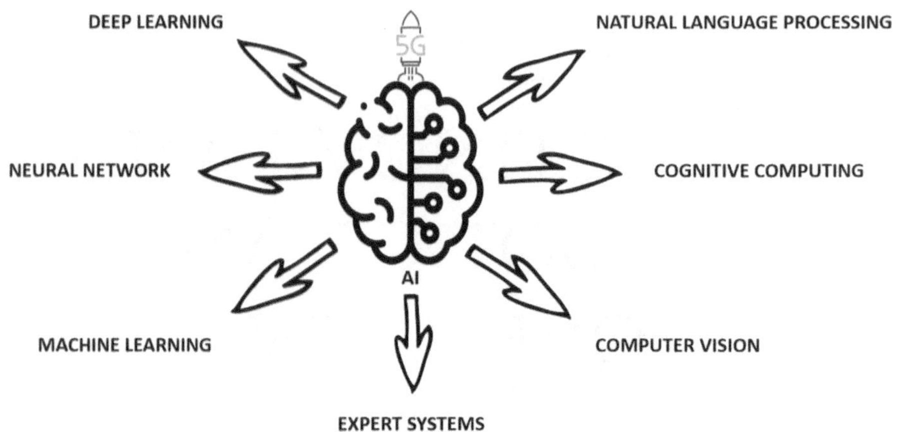

From here on, it's only going to become a more prevalent part of our life; AI will affect our thoughts and behavior, as well as our mental, emotional, and cognitive health. This is just the beginning, with time AI will become more accurate at understanding human thoughts and behavior. And when AI does become more accurate and personalized, it could lead to greater polarization of people, since people with different opinions will see curated content that only validates their opinion.

Our online activities, including social media, are increasingly being customized by AI algorithms to cater to our preferences. As a result, our exposure to different opinions and knowledge is becoming more limited. When we only see posts and comments based on our online history, it can create a paradox.

Let's say you click on a couple of news articles about a recent political event that you feel strongly about; as a result, your entire social media feed will be flooded with posts, opinions, and comments about that topic. You might end up believing the news you're seeing is much bigger than it actually is, keeping you more engaged while also riling up your emotions. Those emotions are what social media companies bank on, to increase your engagement with their platform.

Its partly thanks to 5G and modern chips that companies have the necessary resources to push AI into the mass market, and consumers on the other hand have the power to access AI features thanks to 5G and other upgraded wireless technologies.

Now, robotics is considered one of AI's most influential creations.

The notion of robotics has been present for centuries, albeit in different theories, shapes, and forms. The idea and understanding of robotics evolved hand in hand with the advancements of civilizations. It is only in the past few decades that technology has made significant advancements, allowing us to envision a more defined future for robotics. In the next two decades, we can expect to interact with a wide range of robot types, each with unique capabilities, some practical while others not so practical.

The vision for robotics will remain vague until the industry reaches maturity.

Once the industry reaches a certain level of maturity, possibly around 2045, we can expect robotics to stabilize, similar to how smartphones have mostly stabilized at this point. In the meantime, however, there will always be a general sense of caution among people and society when it comes to emerging industries and revolutionary products, and the industry's reputation can be significantly affected with each failure. This is one of the main reasons why there has been a lack of public demonstrations of robotics, despite the fact that most major tech organizations have been heavily involved in research and development of robotics for the past twenty years.

To give you a better idea, here's an image of different sensors for robotics in comparison to human body:

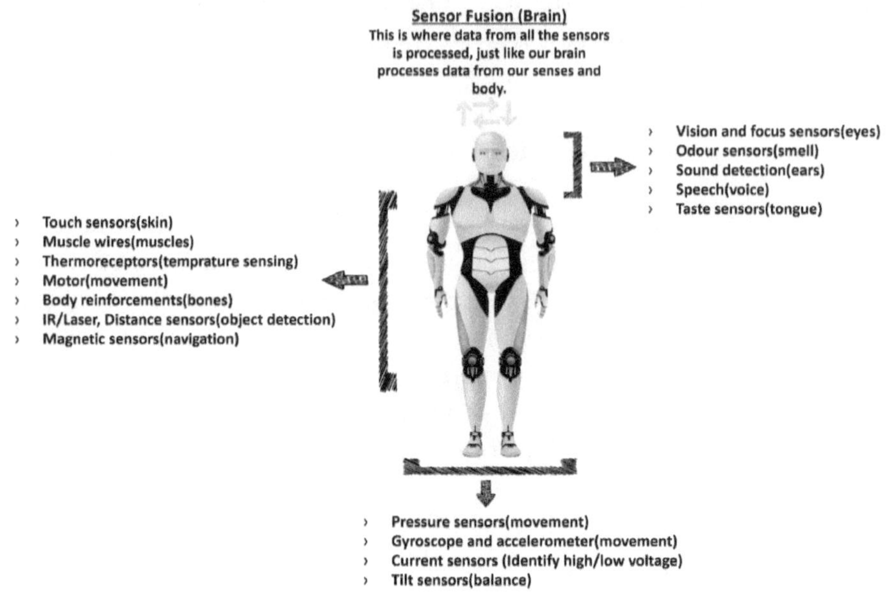

It will take several decades for robots to come anywhere near humans in terms of capabilities, but their programming and design strive to imitate human behavior as closely as possible. With the internet and AI already transforming our world, robotics is positioned to be the next game-changing technology. No matter your location, job, or interests, interacting with robots will eventually become commonplace. They will be a part of almost every industry, spanning across sectors; manufacturing, technology, medical, automotive, mining, construction, banking, education, chemical and any other industry you can think of. It will be there, in one form or another.

As you can see above, to make robots work effectively, there are various technologies at work in tandem. With further advancements in each of these technologies, robots will function even more precisely, reaching closer than ever to human behavior. Leveraging AI's capabilities to solve complex problems is poised to become the primary driving force behind the advancements in robotics.

For example: Recently scientists used AI, specifically deep learning, to make an extraordinary finding - the first new antibiotic compound in nearly 60 years. This remarkable achievement is merely the tip of the iceberg, hinting at a future filled with potential discoveries in the medical field. As hardware technology continues to progress, AI will become increasingly proficient at solving complex problems that would typically require the human mind several decades to solve.

With that in mind, lets talk about theory of mind.

The concept is pretty simple, theory of mind is the ability to understand human emotions, mind, and behavior, that are further divided into 5 stages:

1. Diverse desires
2. Knowledge access
3. Diverse Beliefs
4. False beliefs
5. Hidden emotions

These are the 5 stages of theory of mind and their names are pretty self-explanatory. Understanding each of them is what differentiates a 'human' mind and AI. For robots to exhibit human-like thinking and behavior, it is necessary for them to have a certain level of understanding in all five of these stages, even if not to the fullest extent like a human-brain.

When it comes to AI, theory of mind involves implementation of models that are constructed using data of the various components of human cognition. These models are then integrated into the robot's brain, enabling it to comprehend the behavior and intentions of other sentient creatures. With the models as a starting point, the behavior and response of a robot will dynamically adjust as more data of real world interaction is accumulated. Think of the robot with a new AI model as a 5 year old, who has learned enough about the world to do basic things but not enough to do them well-enough or to form an opinion on the various aspects of human world. From there on, its only forward, as the robot grows older and learns more and more things about our world.

Much like how humans learn and change their perspectives from childhood to adulthood as they learn new things, robots on an individual level can(potentially) develop unique personalities and act on their own after enough exposure to the dynamics of real world.

Conversely, one of the major obstacle to overcome will be ethical behavior. If the robot is consistently subjected to harmful individuals, their ideas, theories, and practices, it has the potential to learn and reproduce those behaviors and thoughts. The challenge lies in preventing this, because any limitations placed on a robot to 'fix' ethical behavior would also hinder its maximum potential. It is worth noting that ethical behavior is a subjective concept and can vary greatly when there are no strong regulations in place from both the industry and government. The ethical aspects of AI and robotics have already become highly debated topics, but so far have failed to gain much attention from either industries or governments.

While theory of mind is still being researched and worked on, it will take a significant amount of time to translate human thoughts, emotions, and behavior into data that can be processed by AI and then executed by robots.

But, there are a lot more concepts working behind-the-scenes.

There is another concept called "Limited Memory". Technologies such as self-driving software, speech recognition, video games, data prediction, IoT devices, and various hardware and software that utilize AI capabilities rely on limited memory.

It functions in a fairly simple manner : it learns from data and adapts accordingly. Imagine you start playing a new sport or video game - you don't have to memorize all the rules beforehand. The first step is to familiarize yourself with the basics, and as you improve your skills and gain experience, you gradually learn all the specific conditions of each rule, and this happens when you face new situations and challenges. Just like that, limited memory starts with the basics and learns as it gathers more data. It uses the accumulated data to enhance predictions, and as it advances, the accuracy of the predictions improve along with it. The advantages of limited memory are evident in self-driving software as it facilitates faster reaction times for the car, utilizing data from vehicles for comprehensive analysis and adaptability. The stored up data helps limited memory to take instant actions based on the past knowledge, just like how humans learn.

Although Cars nowadays collect user data from the infotainment system of each one sold, and training AI is one of the primary reasons behind it. More data = more training for AI*.

*they use your data for a lot of other things once they are done with the training, like selling user data to marketing and insurance companies, you can guess the other ones.

That pretty much sums up the concept of limited memory in AI.

Reinforced learning stands apart from other AI concepts as it can autonomously adapt and learn through interaction. Similar to how humans and animals interact with their surroundings, this sub-field of AI mimics our behavior by utilizing sensors to learn about objects in the environment. Imagine you give a ball to a toddler; he might try to hold it, throw it, or even try to eat it. That's because he is still learning how to interact with new objects, and in the same way; reinforced learning in AI tries different behaviors to learn what's wrong and what's right. The only difference? It has the ability to learn new behavior at a much quicker pace than a child, and without needing constant human guidance. Oh and it doesn't have a fragile body, even if it does risky things and breaks itself you can just transfer the knowledge into a new robot or machine for further growth.

In simpler terms, it relies on trial and error, much like humans, especially kids, do when testing and verifying new knowledge, experiments, and behaviors.

Reinforced learning has wide applications in fields like robotics, financial trading, video games, and resource management including traffic signals and power grids. While reinforced learning has made advancements, it still lags significantly behind when compared to a human brain. Nevertheless, this method is both efficient and adaptable, and as it progresses, we will be closer to achieving machines that can respond and engage in ways similar to humans.

Conversely, narrow AI is highly proficient in specific tasks, but it lacks self-awareness and a deep understanding of its own actions. Among the various types of AI, Narrow AI stands out as one of the most well-known and widely utilized. You may think that this isn't very smart or useful, but even

ChatGPT falls under the category of Narrow AI.

Narrow AI is programmed to handle specific tasks, including image recognition, voice assistant functions, providing recommendations on platforms like Netflix and Amazon, and even predicting weather patterns. However, its functionality is limited to the purpose it was designed for, making it less adaptable than certain other AI concepts.

In the end, there is only one AI that will reign.

Finally, we have Super AI, a concept that, while still in its early stages, will eventually be turned into a tangible technology. The concept, in theory, envisions an AI that surpasses the human mind and its cognitive capacities, pushing the boundaries of possibilities. It will have the ability to make instant decisions after comparing hundreds of outcomes, be self aware, adapt faster than humans, and even have superior processing time and larger data capacity for memory than our brain. It might sound too good to be true, and in some ways, it is. But that's how most technologies sounded in their early stages of concept and development.
Super AI is at a similar stage that AI was in 1956, but within 3 decades, we will have an early version of super AI ready, maybe even earlier depending on how hardware advancements progress in the next 20 years.

The next two decades will shape humanity's future, as newer technologies are implemented and developed at a global scale. Whether the government and society keep up with these rapid changes is yet to be seen, but their roles will be more crucial than ever before. These technologies directly affect human mind, body, and behavior, and at a global scale have the potential to shape not just economy and infrastructure but also opinions. Not just that, but they negatively affect the finite resources that we need for survival, as well as other living creatures.

We'll see how that plays out, but in the meanwhile, lets move on to the next chapter.

CHAPTER TWO

AI IN BUSINESS AND WORKFORCE: A DOUBLE-EDGED SWORD

I've mentioned a few potential professions in this chapter that seem to offer positive prospects for the future. Feel free to skip that section if it doesn't interest you, but I strongly recommend reading just the job names, if nothing else. There are many other things that reading the job names might prompt you to think about, its more like a keyword to get you thinking.

Anyways, lets begin...

In the past 5 years, Artificial Intelligence has played a significant role in the rapid advancement of numerous industries. For AI-based products to work effectively, it is necessary to utilize a wide-range of technologies. The progress and adoption of each of these technologies, individually, will be the key to not only integrating AI into products and services but also for AI to function seamlessly. Since this chapter is geared towards to the effects of AI into our professional lives, I'll be talking more about businesses, industries, and job market.

If you remember, talk of AI started creeping into mainstream media around 2017 with major companies like Samsung, Huawei, Nvidia, Microsoft, and Google perpetually advertising AI based features in their earning reports, events, road-maps, and to consumers. By then, AI and its subsequent technologies had made significant strides in research and development, paving the way for a promising era of growth in the next two decades. These advancements gave companies a clear vision for the future of AI and also reached a level of stability that made them ready for mass public release.

Major tech organizations did this for three key reasons:

1. To get interested and curious customers onboard, so that they hold on to their money for the company to announce future products with more AI implementations. This is done to make sure customers stay interested to invest in the product eco-system of a company
2. To get retail investors interested, create a buzz on social media, and increase speculation, as they might see the new technology as a chance of future wealth growth and hence a good potential for investing into the company.
3. The company aims to secure further investments from long-term investors by showcasing its remarkable progress and ability to expedite product releases. Simultaneously, it seeks to establish itself as an innovative player in the market and actively pursue a larger market share to attract potential large investors.

Sometimes it's a combination of these three, while other times it could be only one or two. In the last two years, from 2021-2023, we've seen companies take more aggressive measures just to woo large shareholders rather than considering all three. **The secret fourth point** would be: when a company is clueless about AI so they just copy the steps of market leaders and hope it works. Like google releasing Gemini before it's fully ready, just to make sure they don't lag behind OpenAI and lose too much of a market share.

More than anything else, the integration of AI into products and services has affected the job market and, as a result, the economy. The job market is directly responsible for a healthy flow of the economy, policy changes, real estate and consumer market; thus, any significant changes to it can have far-reaching consequences, impacting not only an organization but also the entire country and its global trade.

To give you some context:

Let's go back in time to 1990, a time when the internet was still in its early days and companies were contemplating on how to properly utilize this new technology. A period that saw drastic growth of the stock market and valuation of companies were soaring well above their operations, also known as "dot-com bubble". It was in the early 2000s, when businesses started incorporating the internet into their framework to ensure seamless and quick adaptation to future internet changes.

The effectiveness of this method was clearly demonstrated by the achievements of Amazon, E-bay, Netflix, and Google. These companies effortlessly adjusted and kept up with gradual, yet effective, changes in their business model from 2000-2018. They quickly implemented changes to their business and thrivingly kept pace with the rapidly evolving technological landscape, ensuring they stayed competitive.

In the same period of time, several companies failed to accurately gauge and respond to the shifting technology trends. This resulted in the downfall of once-prominent players in their respective industries, including Yahoo, Nokia, Kodak, Xerox, and Blockbuster, who were unable to keep up. Moreover, the collapse of the dot-com bubble in 2000 lead to the closure of many companies, resulting in a substantial unemployment rate. In spite of the bubble burst and the sudden closures that led to widespread job losses, the market not only recovered but also thrived in the subsequent years.
The burst of the bubble acted as a wake-up call for companies, urging them to overhaul their business model and foster a culture of agility to effectively navigate the fast-changing world of technology. Given that the internet was a revolutionary technology, agility was crucial.

In the same way, Artificial Intelligence is yet another revolutionary technology that will compel organizations to rethink their business model, strategy, and hiring process. Evidently so, it is always a struggle to transform an entire company around such drastic changes in technology implementation.

Adapting to change becomes progressively more challenging for larger companies, which is why we often witness a rise in startups whenever a disruptive technology gains widespread acceptance. As businesses vie for market dominance, they are acutely aware that established brands often struggle to keep up with the rapid changes brought about by new technologies, giving start-ups and small companies the edge that they were looking for.

There were multiple layers to the recent degradation of job market and availability:

1. With the lockdowns in place, offices were shut down, manufacturing output was scaled down, and employees had to work remotely. While countries prioritized implementing lockdowns and maintaining hospital capacity, contract workers in industries such as factories, logistics, and construction were disproportionately impacted. They had to wait until lockdown restrictions eased before they could resume earning income, while many others in the service industries were laid off.

2. Following almost a year of the pandemic and remote work, a significant number of employees had an eureka moment; their work doesn't demand as much office presence as they were previously led to believe. The decision to work remotely resulted in time and resource savings for employees. A social media movement emerged where individuals en masse resisted going to the office, hoping to push organizations towards some sort of permanent remote work. However, it presented a major issue for companies as vacant office spaces, especially larger ones, proved to be nothing more than cash burners.

3. Even with reduced production, factories were burning through money by allocating substantial funds towards the upkeep of machinery and logistics. Consequently, many large corporations were overpaying, when compared with production levels, to maintain their supply chain and machinery.

4. Additionally, the construction, hospitality, aviation, and entertainment sectors, as well as retailers struggling with their online presence,

experienced significant repercussions. This had a significant effect on the hundreds of thousands of employees globally, particularly those who lived paycheck to paycheck. With limited job opportunities available for months, a significant number of individuals found it tough to meet their basic needs and had to turn to the government for financial assistance in the form of unemployment benefits.

5. The cost of real estate skyrocketed in numerous countries, causing concerns about a global housing bubble. Evidently so, the real estate market in China experienced a significant crash in the year 2023, resulting in severe economic problems as the country continues to struggle with high rates of youth unemployment.

And here we are now...

The job market is currently bleak due to the inability of economic, employment, education, and global trade policies to keep pace with technological advancements. The pace at which global companies, technology advancements, and technology adoption are evolving exceeds the ability of countries to keep up with new regulations and legislation. The difference in pace among these three factors leads to an imbalance, where companies are constantly promoting new technologies and seeking individuals with the latest skills. However, schools, universities, and skill training programs are not able to match this rapid progress, leaving a considerable number of people with skills that are no longer relevant.

In a survey by intelligent.com, just over 40% business leaders have said that many people graduating in the period of 2019-2024 will graduate with skills that are slowly becoming obsolete. The prolonged period of remote work after the pandemic has raised concerns among business leaders regarding the interpersonal skill development of fresh graduates.

That is how much of an impact AI has inflicted in today's world. Not because its going to take away everything from us, but because it evolves so fast that educational institutions are not able to keep up with AI's pace. Many prominent business leaders fear that over 4 in 10 new graduates, in the past few years as well as in the next few years, will lack skills that are now required by many organizations. Not only that, but due to the pandemic, the emphasis on interpersonal and formal communication has been reduced by many universities.

And it all started with....Covid-19

Which began to spread rapidly, leading to the closure of airports, educational institutes, disruptions in trade, and the enforcement of strict lockdown measures in most countries, effectively suspending more than 60% of businesses. For a duration of no less than eighteen months, this situation persisted, and even though the restrictions were gradually lifted afterwards, the negative impact had already taken its toll.
A decent portion of small and medium companies were sinking & burning cash while others had closed their operations, on the other hand large organizations were acquiring all these collapsing companies or just enjoying the view of lower competition :). Yet, even in the face of major problems, there are always those who identify potential solutions.

Most businesses were still in the transition phase of changing their revenue models; The opportunity of a new disruptive technology was identified by many people globally and thus we saw a surge of startups post 2020. Since large organizations usually take longer to implement these technologies, startups that were designed entirely around leveraging AI found it easier to roll out new products and services as well as making changes to them quicker, based on market trends and customer response.

Established brands wanted more autonomy and had been proactively, and internally, training AI models for many years, in different departments(levels) of their company and had it learn from their own employees until it was fully trained. The lockdown and sudden shortage of workers, forced companies to use the partially trained AI to make up for absence of human resources. Surprisingly, most companies found that the AI models exceeded their expectations and were able to accomplish many repetitive tasks with greater efficiency than humans. Unlike humans, AI does not need breaks and can work non-stop albeit with higher power consumption. Additionally, AI can adapt swiftly and can be easily scaled to meet future growth.

The flexibility of startups and small companies make it easier for them to adapt, as their business and revenue models are not set in stone, enabling their agile business model to evolve and adopt technologies at a faster rate than established and large organizations. During the late 90s and early 2000s, a parallel situation occurred where startups flooded the market en-masse and seized market share of established brands that were too slow to adapt.

Job slowdown, however, is not due to outdated skills...

The reason for the current slowdown in the job market is not entirely a lack of skill-set among individuals, but rather organizations' indecisiveness regarding the implementation of AI and the extent to which it should be implemented in various roles. The introduction of AI in every level of management and business models has led to the obsolescence or gradual elimination of many skills that were traditionally carried out by humans. Consequently, there will be a greater demand for fresh skills to mitigate the new challenges that accompany the extensive implementation of AI. Unfortunately, many individuals above 35 might not *currently* possess those skills, which means they will have to learn new things and practice new skills all over again.

Let's talk about some popular industries, and how they are evolving with this new technology!

<u>**Automobile industry is in a dubious state...**</u>

We've seen a big transformation of products and services in this industry, in the last 6 years. Its not just cars, but trucks, buses, airplanes, bikes, and whatnot. Electric vehicles have also reduced the number of moving parts greatly, reduced from over 200 moving parts to just about 20 on average. This streamlines manufacturing process and reduces the effort required as most of the process can be done by machinery. Electric vehicles require on average 15% less workforce, but require more in battery assembly and manufacturing. Outsourcing batteries allows companies to prioritize skilled workers who can maximize the R&D for future technologies, without having to invest significant amounts of money and human resources into manufacturing batteries.

Again, we see how the workforce is reduced in one department but increased in another. However, both of these require very different Skillset and knowledge. There were over 30,000 layoffs globally in the automotive industry with many of the companies blaming the shift to EV for this. As technology shifts from one to another, the demand for skilled workers in battery manufacturing increases due to the need for expertise in different skills.

However, the issue with this change is that the manufacturing process is being divided among multiple countries. If BMW in Germany chooses to downsize and outsource battery production, factory workers in China will benefit from increased job opportunities, while those laid-off in Europe will need to seek employment elsewhere. As adoption of electric vehicles increase in the next 5 years, more and more companies will slowly reduce their investment into combustion engines. Along with this, the business model and hiring will be designed around the newer products.

Usually, these things have happened throughout history but are more gradual. However, with the sudden rise of semi-conductors, AI, and machine learning, companies are forced to adapt faster than anticipated. Now, major automotive companies are pouring in money to develop and file patents for unique battery technologies that will help them gain greater market share. With EV's, the main focus is on battery range, longevity, and charging speeds. The current state of EV batteries leaves a lot to be desired, when compared to the reliability of combustion cars.

Lobbying technological progress leads to resistance from new entrants...

The influx of new players in the market and the decline in market share and investments of traditional automakers created a sense of panic within the industry. Traditional car companies are playing catch up right now, although they are predicted to catch up and get ahead faster due to their vast resources and industry network.

Again, traditional automakers had been investing and working on electric vehicles for a long time. They were anticipating at least 5-10 years more, before the transition happens, and were rather busy lobbying to delay the push for EV. However, what they didn't predict was that Tesla and Chinese automakers like BYD were already far ahead and streamlined their vehicle lineup, scaling their capacity at a capacity legacy automakers didn't expect.

With the sudden improvements in semi-conductor and battery technologies post 2017, many newer companies realized and saw the potential that traditional automakers were still holding onto and delaying purposefully.

New competition is here

Tesla, lucid motors, Rivian, BYD, Nio, Stellantis, and vinfast have been the biggest winners in the EV push. These companies have received billions in investments and many of them have successfully tested proprietary technologies that they have been working on for years. BYD pioneered battery and semiconductor technologies, as well as their integration into a car.

Today, BYD is the largest EV maker in the world. This is partly thanks to its business of making batteries and assembly of phone components. They entered the solar cell market as well, and are also making chips for their cars. This level of control, and manufacturing all major components of EV indigenously, gave them a humongous advantage while most automakers were lagging years behind in these areas, with tesla being the exception. Tesla's advantage was being the first player and causing a disruption into a traditional market that has historically changed very slowly. Within just years of launching its consumer products for the mass market, tesla became the most valuable car company at $206 billion, surpassing Toyota. Tesla's model 3 was the best selling electric car for 3 years straight, and its success can be credited to the investment into R&D for both automation and its self driving technology.

BYD on the other hand, has been making batteries for decades. They have been in the electric and technology industry for the last few decades while constantly re-investing into R&D for developing cutting edge technology to get ahead of competition. After many years of trial and errors, they finally developed proprietary battery technology which helped them gain an edge over global competition. BYD's blade battery has been talked about a lot, with BYD claiming that their battery technology will fix a lot of major concerns that people have with batteries and electric cars.

Everything is getting a smart screen...

However, with the rise of electric cars, another aspect of the industry has grown tremendously and is the next big focus of many automotive companies: **Software**. Software has become a core part of modern cars and a big selling point for companies, as well as one of the key features that younger consumers look for in a car. Traditionally, every automaker had exclusive software all unique from each other but also pretty basic, in order to differentiate themselves.

Although the features still vary from different models and brands, the gap in software within different brands is much less. Most companies include their exclusive features but also have android auto and apple carplay, both of which can enable the user to run a plethora of features with their phones on every car. This, in turn, streamlines a lot of the user experience for consumers who use cars from different brands.

Seeing this trend, GM announced that it will phase out both android auto and apple carplay from 2024-2025. This news irked a lot of consumers and their families, who are already into the ecosystem of smartphone connectivity. GM claims its own built-in info-tainment system will offer superior user experience, however they have nothing to show for this claim. Many studies and people point out that the switch will instead help GM push its own subscription services to users, and earn more revenue from software.

If this strategy turns out to be successful, it will give automakers complete control over the hardware of car, and what features can a user access. **One such example that happened recently**: BMW had seat ventilation locked behind subscription through their infotainment system. This received a huge backlash from consumers as it appeared that the hardware was already present in the cars but being locked behind software on purpose, and no one wants to pay additional costs after paying a premium for BMW. Subscription services that are locked behind paywalls in cars are often met with disapproval from the majority, as cars are typically seen as a luxury rather than a necessity. Traditionally, cars have always included all the features within the purchasing price rather than being locked by software.

While the subscription strategy has been successful for phones and computers, it does not translate well to the automotive industry, leading to a different perspective and perception. The perception consumers have of an industry, brand, or product is paramount in driving sales. Maintaining this perception and preventing it from declining is a challenging task for companies.

Apple's approach has paid off massively in the last 5 years

Apple, for example, relies heavily on its brand perception by the masses. Iphones in many countries, including the U.S, is seen as a social status and standard among groups of friends or your social network. Apple's value as a company is enhanced by the perception of exclusivity and prestige associated with owning their products.
It takes a lot of work to uphold that level of perception and brand image, and Apple is the only tech company that has been successful in continuously retaining repeat customers and drawing in new ones. Maintaining a steady rise in wealth and sales, even after achieving the position of one of the most valuable companies globally, is no small accomplishment. (Except for the constant buybacks aimed at increasing share value to meet quarterly bonuses.)

<u>How market leaders fell prey to their own success</u>

The story of market leaders, including Nokia, serves as a cautionary tale, reminding us that maintaining a dominant position in the market requires continuous adaptation and evolution to keep up with the rapid pace of competition.

Nokia's downfall can be attributed to several factors

1. Firstly, their management's refusal to innovate and adapt their products was a major contributor. For years, they tried pushing their own OS but implemented it poorly. Nokia's symbian OS had huge potential to compete with IOS and Android, but they took it slowly and didn't aggressively push for its development. Giving competitors a lot of time to catch up.
2. They underestimated the rapid pace of change in the industry. When you've been the market leader for so many years, companies become more relaxed and think they can just adapt later due to their vast

resources and network. But, they forget that implementation and allocation of resources is more important than merely hoarding it.

3. The emergence of new competitors and disruptors caught them off guard, coupled with their overestimation of customer loyalty. Customer loyalty is rare in the tech industry, even when it comes to high-end products. Because it is relatively simple to switch between different products, many consumers possess a range of smart devices from various brands that align with their variety of preferences and needs.

Today, the smart-phone market is witnessing fierce competition as Apple, Samsung, Huawei, and Xiaomi are aggressively pushing their eco-systems, which include an extensive array of products ranging from smartwatches, speakers, tags, earbuds, and smart-lights to TV's and cars. This extensive lineup has prompted many to categorize these offerings under the umbrella of the **"smart-home"** ecosystem.

Nokia, Htc, Blackberry, Yahoo, Kodak, Xerox - once giants in their industries - now serve as cautionary tales of the perils of complacency, their lack of innovation and poor decision making, leaving them vulnerable to the ever-advancing competition.

For any brand to thrive, it is imperative that they embrace innovation as a fundamental aspect of their business strategy. This entails reinvesting a significant portion of their revenue into research and development to ensure they are well-equipped to tackle unforeseen industry changes. Whether it be technological advancements, policy shifts, organizational structure, or the emergence of disruptive competitors with novel technologies, companies must be prepared to adapt and evolve.

Leadership is equally important; IBM and Xerox for example, had developed a variety of personal computers but didn't believe in the technology to be successful enough and ended up abandoning their product line, giving competitors that were still behind an advantage.

The technology industry, especially mass-market products, only last so long. The competition is so cut-throat that new companies keep entering and trying to disrupt with their implementation of technology, as well as established brands experimenting and adding new products and features every year to one-up each other. Although, as of 2024, that is not the case anymore. Samsung and Apple are trade partners, and are working together to push for a duopoly by both pushing similar features and prices, to slowly drive up costs and make their services a standard in the industry for most people. This is what we call **'market shaping'**.

You get a subscription plan, you get one too, and you too!

Services on the other hand, including software, applications, and cloud, are an entirely different story. They are harder to penetrate by new entrants, costlier, but also have higher loyalty than hardware based products. Apple was the first company to majorly invest in their services and eco-system, it took them years of re-investing a huge chunk of profits but it finally paid off. Many other companies finally caught on; with how much profits can be made from services, and started entering the software market.

Apple services in 2023 earnings report noted 23.1 billion in revenue, above the estimates, while samsung reported 14 billion in sales of its cloud services in 2022. The costs for managing(or fees if you outsource) cloud services on such a large scale, however, are high. This creates a barrier for smaller and newer companies to enter the competition among established brands.
This, in turn, becomes a positive for established brands as it generates an added value for customers by offering exclusive services based on cloud and AI, thereby encouraging customers to remain loyal and continue purchasing hardware from the same brand. With this method, these established brands have created some level of customer loyalty in the tech market, where loyalty otherwise is pretty low.

Cloud based services saw a boom in recent years due to AI and semiconductor improvements. Hardware capable enough to leverage AI features was the final push needed to make AI mainstream and add it to every smart-device possible.
One of the reasons for the consistent success of companies like Samsung and LG in the appliance market is their extensive research and development efforts, expertise in software from their phone division, along with their ability to effectively integrate software into their products. Unlike many other companies that rely on partnering with software

companies to incorporate AI and smart features into their products, these companies, being self-reliant, have a significant advantage.

The automobile industry is the next big market to penetrate for chip makers, as well as for apple and google, to sell their cloud and app based services, in some cases also providing android OS designed specifically for cars. For car companies however, using software and features from either Apple or Google would mean having less control over what customers can and cannot access. That is why, many automobile companies are hiring engineers to develop their own OS. Having their own OS will give them complete control over the car, which will then help them to sell more services and lock features behind subscriptions.

On one hand we have Tesla, that has been providing their full self-driving access behind subscriptions, and to some extent it is working quite well for them. Since the self-driving software is still in early stages and requires constant R&D, this makes sense to both the company and customers, but for standard hardware features that have been traditionally provided for free; customers expect to pay for it upfront when they pay for the car. Majority of the current consumer demographics have not shown any interest in subscription based features for cars, hence the entire industry will be watching carefully about how it progresses with GM's approach.

Automobile companies are playing the long game

Despite this, there is another element to these sudden changes. The goal is to gradually incorporate these changes into cars, ensuring that by the time today's younger generation, who will be the future target market, comes of age, they will already be accustomed to subscription-based services in other products as well. It's like conditioning you, gradually shaping your habits and thoughts until your purchasing preferences align with their business model.

And that is why raising awareness about these changes becomes so important!

The presence of subscription services on our phones, computers, TVs, and various appliances is causing a shift in consumer behavior, as more people are accepting the idea of paying for services that were once bundled with the product. The automobile industry is eagerly awaiting the widespread acceptance of subscription-based models. Once this trend becomes the norm, major companies will join forces and implement subscription plans that lock essential features behind paywalls. As a result, customers will be left with no choice but to subscribe to one of the available options.

Once this happens, there will be a corresponding shift in hiring. With the changing product and service offerings of companies, there will be a major shuffle in investment distribution; leading to changes in employee requirements.

Skill demand is changing globally

The changing demand for skills is leaving many recent graduates with obsolete skills and increasing the demand for different or newer skills. Universities and people were caught off guard by the sudden shift in skill demands. The process of updating university courses to align with industry requirements usually takes a few years, as subjects are gradually added or removed.
However, the rapid advancement of AI occurred in just two years, coinciding with the peak of the pandemic when many institutions were struggling to operate effectively. This further hindered the process of adapting new skills into university courses. According to experts, individuals who have graduated, and even those who will graduate in 2025, may face significant challenges in the future as the demand for skills undergoes a drastic transformation.

But it's not all gloomy. There are a lot of skills that can be learned regardless of your history in education and work experience, especially since the next decade will see a drastic shift in economy, technology and business structure.

Here are some potential jobs that seem to have a rather positive outlook, based on the current trends:

1. **Programming languages** such as Java, Python, C++ , and C will remain in a consistent demand going into 2030. But, languages such as Kotlin, Swift, Rust, and Scala will see an incremental growth in demand as AI, data science, and app based services increase. With Google and Apple focus on making app development more efficient, languages like Kotlin and Swift

will thrive.

Although the future of coding is vague, CEO of Nvidia said "coding will die and be automated, so youth should focus on upskilling". It seems like he is unsure himself about what upskilling here refers to, considering that his idea of upskilling involves farming. Despite that, my opinion remains that entry-level programming jobs will cease to exist as AI continues to progress and automate coding. But mid-level and senior level positions will be constantly hired, maybe in lower numbers than before. While the exact timeframe remains unclear, my prediction is that the demand for these skills will persist at-least until 2035, particularly due to the continued hiring of programmers by small and medium-sized companies. As well as for maintaining the current systems that will remain in operation for at least another decade.

With the industry's adoption of data science, AI, and machine learning, the demand for workers with expertise in these fields will soar. According to current estimates, programming languages are expected to experience a 10-15% global growth over the next 7 years. However, this estimate is subject to change if there are any significant technological disruptions, but a decline is unlikely. Considering the global prevalence and spread of programming as a profession, the seemingly modest 15% increase in this field is actually quite significant in numbers and should not be underestimated.

2. The **renewable energy** sector is expected to experience a significant surge in both demand and growth, making it another industry to keep a close eye on. While there are specific degrees in renewable energy, having any degree can greatly enhance one's prospects in the field of renewable energy; even though it may involve a steeper learning curve for additional skills. By 2030, the renewable energy industry is projected to create more than 40 million jobs worldwide, depending on each country's commitment to renewable energy adoption.

Renewable energy specialists are responsible for a wide range of tasks, including:

1.   Designing and developing renewable energy systems.
2.   Installing and maintaining renewable energy equipment.

3. Conducting research and development on new renewable energy technologies.
4. Educating the public about renewable energy.
5. Advocating for renewable energy policies.
6. Renewable energy consultant, and sales representative.
7. Project developer and manager within a company.
8. Renewable Energy Permitting Specialist

Outside of renewable energy industry, the demand for renewable energy specialists is expected to grow in all sectors of the economy, including:

- Electric power generation.
- Transportation.
- Manufacturing.
- Construction.
- Agriculture.

3. The **blockchain industry** is experiencing rapid expansion. While blockchain is frequently associated with cryptocurrency, its applications extend far beyond that. Essentially, blockchain is a database system that enables smooth data sharing within a business network. True to its name, it stores data by linking multiple blocks together. Consequently, these blocks of data are rendered more secure.

The use of blockchain is present across industries such as renewable energy, finance, media, and retail. Just like other industries, the blockchain industry is also expected to witness a significant growth, with projections indicating that over 1 million jobs will be created and 40 million directly/indirectly influenced by blockchain until 2030. As a result, regions such as the US, European Union, and the Middle East will experience a surge in demand for blockchain technology.

4. Despite being well-established careers, **cyber security and ethical hacking** will experience a surge in demand in the coming decades; due to the growing reliance on technology by both companies and individuals, cybersecurity is expected to undergo significant expansion in the coming years.
Data will become increasingly valuable over the next twenty years. With

its expansion, the requirement for consistently enhancing and upkeeping security will also surge. According to projections, the growth of the cybersecurity sector is expected to surpass 30% with an average growth rate of 14%, making it one of the fastest-growing industries.

5. Experts predict a substantial growth of 25-30% for **AI prompt engineering** by 2030. The rising popularity of artificial intelligence (AI) and machine learning (ML) applications is driving this trend. Developing and refining prompts for AI and ML models falls under the responsibility of prompt engineers. Their contribution is vital in making sure that these models can generate accurate and relevant results.
Engineers who possess a strong background in AI, ML, and NLP will find themselves in high demand. Some other bonus skills would be to not only have decent communication and problem-solving skills but also to be able to collaborate effectively with others.

6. **Autonomous car mechanic:** The increasing prevalence of autonomous vehicles means that there will be a greater need for mechanics who possess the necessary skills to service and fix them. To excel as autonomous car mechanics, individuals must possess a solid grasp of electrical and computer systems. Moreover, they must be capable of diagnosing and fixing intricate mechanical issues, and be well-versed in the software systems employed by different brands. Several factors are contributing to the positive job prospects for autonomous car mechanics.

These factors include:

- The increasing software complexity of automobiles.
- The growing popularity of autonomous vehicles.
- The aging workforce of automotive mechanics.
- The need for more specialized skills to maintain and repair autonomous vehicles, such as understanding and working with the various sensors all the different cars will have. Since even a small error during servicing can render some sensors useless.

7. **Augmented reality journey builder:** The Bureau of Labor Statistics (BLS) projects that employment of "multimedia designers and animators" will grow 4% from 2020 to 2030. As technology adoption and prevalence

increases, so will the demand for employees to develop and maintain these futuristic gadgets.

This growth is due to the increasing demand for AR applications in a variety of industries, including:

1. Retail: AR can be used to help customers visualize products in their homes or businesses before they buy them.
2. Education: AR can be used to create immersive learning experiences that bring history, science, and other subjects to life.
3. Manufacturing: AR can be used to help workers visualize complex assembly procedures and troubleshoot problems.
4. Healthcare: AR can be used to provide patients with information about their medical conditions and procedures.
5. Gaming is another industry that will use this technology, possibly more than many others. AR journey builders will need to have a strong understanding of AR technology, as well as the ability to design and develop AR experiences.

Some of the skills that AR journey builders will need:

1. 3D modeling and animation: AR journey builders will need to be able to create 3D models and animations that can be used in AR applications.
2. Programming: AR journey builders will need to be able to program AR applications using a variety of programming languages.
3. User experience (UX) design: AR journey builders will need to be able to design AR experiences that are user-friendly and engaging.
4. Creativity: AR journey builders will need to be creative in order to come up with new and innovative AR applications. Platforms like Unity, ARKit , ARCore, Vuforia are commonly used to build AR experiences.

8. The demand for **data science** has increased in the last three years and is expected to continue growing as AI and data science become more prevalent in various industries. The Bureau of Labor Statistics (BLS) projects that employment of data scientists will grow 13% from 2022 to 2032. However, the 13% is only for the US market, in other major regions such as the EU, China, India, Japan, Korea, and UAE, these jobs will see a

rise as well.

This growth is being driven by the increasing demand for data-driven decision-making in a variety of industries, including:

- Technology: Data scientists are needed to develop and implement machine learning algorithms, analyze large datasets, and build predictive models.
- Healthcare: Data scientists are needed to analyze patient data, identify trends, and work with others to develop new methods.
- Finance: Data scientists are needed to analyze market data, develop trading strategies, and manage risk.
- Retail: Data scientists are needed to analyze customer data, identify trends, and develop personalized marketing campaigns.
- Manufacturing: Data scientists are needed to analyze sensor data, identify defects, and improve production processes.

9. **3D modeling** is an industry that is growing quickly, and the job market for 3D modelers is looking very favorable. The Bureau of Labor Statistics (BLS) projects that employment of 3D modelers will grow by 15% from 2020 to 2030. Again, since this data is only for the US, other major economies will also see a rise in demand for these skills. Some applications of it are:

- Video games: 3D models are used to create the characters, environments, and objects in video games.
- Movies and television: 3D models are used to create the characters, sets, and special effects in movies and television shows.
- Architecture and engineering: 3D models are used to design buildings, bridges, and other structures.
- Manufacturing: 3D models are used to design and prototype products.
- Medical imaging: 3D models are used to create images of the human body that can be used to diagnose diseases and plan treatments.
- 3D modelers with a strong background in art, design, and computer science will be in high demand. They should also have strong communication and problem-solving skills.

10. **Climate change mitigation** specialists will experience significant growth as this field has been largely overlooked in the past. In the near future, the problem of climate change will become even more prominent. As countries continue to pass legislation for environmental preservation, the demand for individuals in this role extends beyond renewable energy companies.

Some of the major industries that will hire for this role are:

1. Government agencies
2. NGO's
3. All manufacturing companies, across industries. Such as: textile, consultation firms, FMGC, Chemicals, Machinery, etc.
4. Tech companies; since AI requires a large amount of resources to run.

Their roles, not limited to, include:

1. Policy formation
2. Educating target audience about environmental impacts
3. Research and analysing data
4. Project development
5. Working with other departments to effectively reduce the climate impact of a company.

11. **Urban agriculture** has huge potential for several reasons. As more and more greenland is destroyed for meeting the growing human consumption needs, urban agriculture will become extremely important. One of the most popular aspects of urban agriculture is vertical farming. But anyways, without agriculture humans cannot survive. Large scale agriculture is essential for human surviving, and thus agriculture will move from the vast lands to urban infrastructure, and many other new innovate applications.

Some forms of urban agriculture include:

1. Vertical farming
2. Hydroponics and Aquaponics
3. Street farming

4. Backyard farming
5. Urban beekeeping
6. Rooftop gardens/farming

And that is, potentially, what a big part of future tech job market could look like...

Sustainable manufacturing and development will be one of the key point of highlight in the future, and almost all companies will look to hire for this role. However, many will also do it simply to put on a facade. In a recurring pattern throughout history, organizations hire individuals to gather sustainability data, but ultimately dissolve the department and suppress any resulting reports. **Uhm don't search 'Exxon Mobil climate change report 1977' on google...**

The decision to hire individuals for showing on paper serves a dual purpose of enhancing their marketing strategies for improving their acceptance by the general public and ensuring they remain in compliance with government regulations. However, implementing these changes to actually improve sustainability is an entirely different story. Regardless, most jobs will continue to evolve and make use of advanced technologies. Automation could potentially replace a multitude of mundane tasks, while simultaneously introducing new tasks/skills to existing roles within an organization.

Over the next twenty years, the business of data selling and mining is set to become one of the largest and most profitable industries, with Meta, X, Google, Amazon, Microsoft, and Apple positioned to be the biggest beneficiaries. These companies have a significant global user base and gather extensive user data, which is then utilized to support their AI projects. Examples of AI applications include generative AI for file creation, AI in cameras, and software that uses AI to make data-based predictions. Don't limit your understanding of data to just numbers; it can encompass wide range of forms such as images, audio, videos, text, biometrics, and even just basic usage pattern. Every software and hardware can benefit from getting trained on data, but only if it used for ethical purposes, and not for other shenanigans.

The impact on people and society

Since the year 2020, there has been a significant transformation in the outlook for both companies and individuals in terms of jobs. Many companies are eliminating jobs and streamlining their business processes as they strive for complete automation. The recent years, 2022 and 2023, have shown a clear pattern of waves of layoffs, leading many to believe that the market was finally stabilizing now(in 2024). However, to our surprise, since the start of 2024, there have been over 100,000 layoffs globally and we haven't even reached the halfway mark yet. We can expect an increase in layoffs in the upcoming months as more companies are announcing job cuts every quarter to meet the goal of ceo and exec bonuses in their financial reports.

The realization that humans are considered dispensable resources, especially by large-scale organizations, creates an overwhelming sense of desperation among a lot of employees. It's not uncommon for them to receive hundreds, if not thousands, of applications for each position they advertise. The result of this is an unequal distribution, whereby the company assumes a position of superiority and has the freedom to terminate and choose individuals as they please. This allows them to hire and fire employees as they please, without any consideration for their expectations.

As AI continues to advance and improve in its capabilities, humans are increasingly seen as a liability. Executives and board members are fond of machines because they can work tirelessly, have no emotional or personal needs, and obediently follow every command. Their perfect idea of what an employee should be. While the initial expenses are greater and the maintenance requires specific expertise for each machine and software, the benefit lies in the relentless and uninterrupted performance of these programs and machines, as they are capable of accomplishing a wide range of tasks.
Looking at it from the perspective of a profit-driven company, this option appears to be worth the inconvenience of a significant initial investment. But as a human, it seems poisonous for the stability of a healthy and sustainable future.

Unstable employee retention rate is another factor.

It's not only about productivity, but machines and programs provide long-term stability and reassurance for companies. The employee turnover and retention rate can be quite unpredictable due to various factors such as market conditions and the growth of competitors. In these circumstances, employees may choose to switch companies either for a higher salary or to pursue a different role. The ability to retain talent ultimately depends on which company is able to offer greater benefits and rewards to its skilled employees. Although everything appears joyful, the happiness is fleeting and relies solely on the company's continuous growth. Once the growth begins to decelerate, those workers become burdensome as they require constant financial and other incentives in the form of rewards. On the other hand, a lot of employees use these companies as a stepping stone to constantly switch jobs for several different reasons.

Apart from legal issues, the time and resources required for continuous employee training, which may involve significant investments with no guarantee of long-term employee loyalty. When this occurs, companies find themselves wasting their resources and investments, necessitating either a repetition of the process with new employees or the hiring of individuals at a higher compensation. While these choices may not be morally or ethically ideal, they are often addressed in quarterly reports within a company, especially when the company is facing financial losses or when there are alternatives for achieving profitability.

These statements might hold some truth, but it is not always in the company's best interest to prioritize them. When major technological changes occur within an industry, some organizations opt to reassign their employees and provide them with training for acquiring new skills. It is important to acknowledge that the success of these decisions is not always clear-cut and depends largely on the judgment of those responsible for making them. It's never black or white, or as simple as just hiring or firing. There are several different forces at play, with different solutions, fighting to implement what they want.

CHAPTER THREE

MODERN APPLICATIONS FOR A MODERN APPROACH

How can we strive in these times of a major technological shift in almost every industry and role?

The answer is not as simple as finding a single way out; it's a complex puzzle with multiple paths to consider. The market is currently shapeless, like a river flowing through a rocky terrain, constantly changing its course as external forces shape its direction. It will take time for the market to find stability, like how the river eventually settles into a steady flow. As the waves change in direction and intensity, all those residing in that body of water will continue to be affected. What we can do, though, is get ready for the unknown future by enhancing our skills. Similar to how we frequently update our tech gadgets, such as smartphones and laptops, to access new features and to get the latest features that would enhance our life. So, all we need to do is upgrade ourselves. Easy peasy, especially for humans, who are considered as the dominant species with the most complex brain on earth.

These points will just be a foundation to do things your way. **To illustrate:** once you have acquired the ability to walk, running becomes a natural extension of that skill. In the same way, 'upskilling' our life is just an upgrade to our foundation, rather than learning something that is completely alien to us.

Now let's talk about some useful software products that can be used for productivity:

OFFICE SUITE

Regardless of your occupation or industry, there is one tool that is used by everyone. Let's start with that. Microsoft Office and Google Workspace are the two leading options in this category. For many years, Microsoft Office has been the go-to platform for creating documents, giving presentations, and managing data in Excel. Over the past 10 years, Google Workspace has made remarkable strides in gaining a strong foothold in the market.

1. For small and medium companies, and startups, google workspace is seen as a better option, since it is not only easier to adopt for new users, but also cheaper at a per user price. Gmail's popularity as the most widely used email service makes integration effortless and provides users with cloud storage across all Google apps, not limited to the Google Office suite.

2. Statistically, Google workspace has a higher rate of users working on the same document, at the same time i.e. collaborative use. Almost 85% of users have collaborated on google workspace apps simultaneously, while it's only 68% for Microsoft office suite. Real-time data collaboration is considered a significant driver of productivity, particularly in meetings. However, the absence of such collaboration often leads to decreased productivity as contributions and input from individuals are frequently delayed or overlooked.

The significance of collaboration among employees from diverse levels and departments, particularly in the context of data and record sharing, cannot be overstated as it allows everyone to strive towards a shared goal. Moreover, this fosters a perception that people's viewpoints and recommendations are being captured and valued in meetings, potentially leading to increased productivity on an individual basis. While it may not be true for everyone, some employees prioritize collaboration over other aspects. Thus, google workspace is a great tool for many, especially start-ups and small businesses, due to its ease of use and integration with other google services.

***Do note that since Google workspace is used more by smaller organizations, where hierarchy is less prevalent, the collaboration**

rates automatically become higher regardless of the software used.

3. Where Microsoft *excels*, however, is functionality. It has the greatest functionality of any office suite, period. For large organizations and companies, these are essential, since the amount of data they work with requires an application that can handle and process it, without causing constant issues or crashes. Features such as formatting and analysis tools are better in office 365. As for excel and data processing, there is no competition. It's the industry standard for managing all kinds of data across departments.

4. Yet, another minor advantage Microsoft 365 has; integration with windows OS. A lot of features seamlessly integrate with 365. And with the rise in co-pilot features, Microsoft 365 will gain even more AI features baked directly into the OS for quick and seamless feature compatibility and data transfer.

These fundamentals are becoming even more important with the emergence of AI-powered chatbots such as ChatGPT and Google Gemini. As a result, AI integration is being implemented across office suites to enhance their capabilities and perform a wide range of tasks. And here's why it matters - these changes will totally change the skills needed for a lot of jobs. With the improvements in AI, an increasing number of intricate tasks that once demanded humans to execute convoluted formulas and functions can now be automated and accomplished by individuals (or programs) with lesser proficiency in those particular skills. With AI taking care of everything, all you need is a simple User Interface to control it.

For example: Co-pilot in Microsoft 365 offers a lot of features that had to be previously done manually.

Features like:

1. In word, it can **create, summarize, comprehend, refine, and elevate your documents**. Now you can use enhanced capabilities like visualizing and transforming text into a table. Some other capabilities also include adding onto existing prompts, drafting a document by referencing up to 3 documents and discovering information about your document.

2. Copilot in PowerPoint helps you turn your ideas into stunning presentations. As your storytelling partner, Copilot can transform existing written documents into decks complete with speaker notes and sources or start a new presentation from a simple prompt or outline. Condense lengthy presentations at the click of a button and **use natural language commands** to adjust layouts, reformat text, and perfectly time animations.

3. Copilot in Excel Highlight, filter, and sort your data. **Data analysis and visualization**: Copilot can highlight trends, perform calculations, and suggest data visualizations, assisting you in understanding and presenting your data effectively. **Formula suggestion and error detection**: It can recommend relevant formulas based on your data and detect potential errors, ensuring accuracy and efficiency in your spreadsheets. **Interactive charts and dashboards**: Copilot can create interactive charts and dashboards from your data, making it easier to share insights and engage your audience.

4. For outlook, **Email writing and scheduling**: Copilot can help you craft concise and impactful emails, suggesting different tones and phrasing options. It can also schedule emails and calendar appointments for you, streamlining your communication. **Meeting summaries and action items**: After a meeting, Copilot can automatically generate a summary of key points and discussion topics, along with suggested action items and deadlines, ensuring clarity and follow-through. **Smart search and information retrieval:** It can quickly find relevant information and emails within your inbox, allowing you to easily retrieve the information you need.

5. Copilot in Loop helps you unlock the power of shared thinking - **co-create, get up-to-speed, and stay in sync with your co-workers.** Now you can iterate with Copilot collaboratively as a team, co-creating prompts, generating tables to help organize team projects, catch up where your teammates left off, summarize page content, and generate a recap for a teammate you're handing work off to.

And it's not just Microsoft 365; popular apps like zoom, teams, Canva, Photoshop etc. are all adding more and more AI based features. While products like Mural, Jira, and confluence flaunt their AI features openly, and even promote their integration with software like Microsoft 365 and Canva.

GENERATIVE AI- ENDLESS POSSIBILITIES

Just like how ChatGPT and other AI chatbots are all the fad today, generative AI is the next darling of consumer industry. Generative AI is 'generating' things by using machine learning models to identify patterns and co-relate between those patterns in order to predict and create things like images, videos, music, and more. That's why popular productivity and editing apps like Adobe Photoshop and office 365 are constantly adding and improving generative AI integration.

For example: You can now replace background, add/remove objects and fill image data just by using AI, as compared to manually starting from scratch in pre-ai era. Not only that, you can use AI for object selection, image blending, precise hair selection, and even give you a step by step guide for how to perform certain actions, which is very useful for beginners. As time goes on, these features will get more accurate and new features based on generative AI will be added.

Not to scare you or anything, but we even have eye contact correction using AI. You can be looking somewhere else during a video call, and the other person would still see your eyes glazing towards the screen. This is a really handy feature, especially for those annoying work calls where everyone is just yapping.

Amidst all this, as individuals, what we can do is to gain an understanding of how these features operate and store that knowledge in our little brain, since most software products will integrate AI regardless of you liking it or not. The sooner we become familiar with them, the more advantageous it will be.

The game of getting your Resume noticed by AI overlords

Generative AI can be used to make attractive resumes and cover letters. However, in today's world, the text within a resume holds far greater importance than its visual aesthetics. For most job positions that are opened, especially those available in large organizations, the competition is fierce, with thousands of applicants vying for the same opportunity from all around the country, if not the globe. It is rare for a human to review the first stage of submitting resumes and cover letters online, as it is logistically impossible. While traditionally, most of the job applications were handled by humans, today its mostly automated and will keep getting even more automated as AI gets better at its job.

Sorting through resumes is a common task for medium and large organizations, and to streamline this process, they utilize different software applications that come with diverse settings and personalization options. These software programs are designed to scan the text within the resumes. In order to find the most relevant information, the software searches for keywords that have been rated according to their importance (by the organization you're applying to). Moreover, any keywords that have been blacklisted by the organization will prompt the software to automatically send a rejection email :(

And this is where modern 'AI' comes into play, there is nothing better than an 'AI' based software to counter the filtering software of organizations. Today, a large chunk of the application process relies more on who can crack the loopholes in software filtering and get their applications noticed by the AI overlords.

So lets get down to the focus points:

With ChatGPT/Gemini, you have the ability to leverage its capabilities for multiple tasks related to job applications. For instance, you can utilize it to compose a well-crafted cover letter and resume. What's more, you can compare the job requirements to your existing resume and make necessary updates by emphasizing the essential skill keywords required for the position. **For example:** "Can you tell me the important skills for x job?" or "can you tell me what skills/keywords should I mention in my resume for x job?". Something along those lines, you can get creative with the questions to get the answers you seek.

If we can't beat AI on our own, we should look for ways to use AI for beating AI

We can even rely on ChatGPT/Gemini to assist you in drafting an email for applications, tailored specifically to the job requirements. While it's pretty obvious that you shouldn't hit send on that email just by copy/pasting, you can definitely use it as a foundation to create your own email.

You can try something like "can you write an email format for job application?" or "can you write an email for applying to a marketing job/role?". You can experiment with posing questions in different ways, resulting in varied responses and insights. By including certain job requirements in your questions, you can make the email more tailored to your needs.

So this is how it goes:

You can use ChatGPT to get job interview questions related to your job, get a mock interview style questionnaire, and even get an introduction for yourself, based on your resume and your job requirements. You'll get all the public data on your screen, so you won't have to waste time searching for each point individually.

If you're already working on something, you can use these chatbot AI's to get new ideas for your brainstorming sessions. For example, you can write "give me different perspectives/approach for x idea or to solve x problem". Both ChatGPT and Gemini will then give answers to your ideas, with things such as legal, social, global perspectives for implementing your ideas, and sometimes even out of the box (unconventional) ideas. It can also give you an outline, summary, and bullet points for your brainstorming session.

You could summarize your reports and documents, granted you don't upload any sensitive company data online and leak it accidentally (**oops!**). I mean, some people have done that even in companies like Amazon, where employees were later banned from uploading documents on ChatGPT. You'd expect people working in a supposedly e-commerce business would know about it. But you can remove the sensitive data and copy/paste the text into a new file, to help you summarize and refine your reports and projects. It not only helps with language and improving the flow of topics, but also give you information based on the latest news and trends with relation to that topic. But, Microsoft office and many other office suites have built-in summarization, with better privacy.

Researching statistics, data, and finding research material has never been easier. Leveraging ChatGPT and Gemini can help us in searching the entire web for data, instead of manually looking up each website. You can also ask the AI chatbot to provide sources and summaries both, which you can then lookup manually, if you find relevant information. You can look up research papers as well, which will then help you in being more efficient and be more productive? Or be lazier. Depending on your personality...

More uses...

- This is one of the best uses for these new AI chatbots; creating presentations and reports. You can use Microsoft 365, Canva, and other online tools to create visually stunning designs for presentations and reports, and then modify those with your relevant data. They can create presentations of different styles, different moods, and for different reasons i.e. both casual and formal. All of them use either a custom api from GPT or Gemini. And all you have to do is just enter text about how you want the presentation to look like.
- Creating a to-do list for your daily tasks is easier than ever, and you can also use these chatbots for creating a financial planning framework/ layout and then allot your budget on it. This helps in learning your spending habits and different ways to use your money more effectively in different parts of your lives.
- Learning new skills and knowledge has become easier. ChatGPT and Gemini can give you latest information on almost any topic, and also recommend you latest resources based on your preferences. You can do this frequently in your free time, to make sure you're up-to-date with the latest topics and trends in your field of work and not left behind when there are new major changes in your line of work. You can also use them to learn about various policies and law changes in relation to your industry, this can be very useful especially if you're planning for a career change in the future and looking to upgrade yourself for it.

Now this is something many of you might know, ChatGPT and Gemini can be used to write code and scripts. But there are limits to what it can and cannot do.

1. Writing code blocks in languages like python, Java, C++, C, Javascript,

SQL, and more. These snippets can then be used in your program or project, along with the other code you've written. Although it's best to modify the code, as it may not always be completely functional, but it will provide you with a clearer image on how to write code for the next part. This is especially useful for people who are learning or are fairly new to programming, this gives you a somewhat accurate code to work with, if you're bad at starting from scratch and want to grow your skills.

2. It can also be used for defining functions within the code and getting suggestions for missing parts in the code, syntax, and for potential debugging. Although its not 100% accurate, it can still help in scanning large amounts of code to look for patterns of missing pieces, which could otherwise take much longer.

3. Lastly, it can also be used to convert your code into another programming language. This is useful if you've already written a large amount of code. You can then manually correct the fixes on the translated code, since there are bound to be some errors created in translation. These chatbots can also create code from descriptions of your desired functionality from a set of code.

But, for things that it, currently, cannot do:

It still has a limited understanding of complex codes and languages. For example: algorithms, data structures, and complex concepts confuse the poor little brains of ChatGPT and Gemini. Sadly, that will only last for so long, as time passes and they get older, their brains will grow too. It's like watching your child grow into an adult.

Since we're on this topic, these chatbots cannot handle large amounts of code either. **Such as**; large applications and systems with intricate logic and dependencies. Although, we will have dedicated softwares leveraging that aspect for AI just for programming, in the future. We have many organizations working on training GPT and Gemini models to create accurate codes, how long that takes is yet to be seen. In the beginning, training should be relatively easy, but as the code expands and becomes more intricate, achieving accuracy will become significantly more challenging.

Because the code generated by GPT and Gemini have flaws and errors, they are not practical for creating independent programs capable of running on their own. They require human oversight and interference at every step to make sure there are no stones left unturned, especially in code blocks for a large project.

Even though ChatGPT and Gemini can do so many things, much faster than most people, its still in its early stages. Within the next decade, its going to improve drastically and at an exponential rate. AI, currently, is going to see slow growth for a while, but once the it gathers enough data from around the world, its going to have an exponential growth. And this is why AI can threaten a lot of human jobs, in regular intervals for the next three decades at least. Not because of it's ability to process a lot of information within minutes, but because after a certain period of time it will always see an exponential improvements due to the large amounts of data that is gathered globally.

Once AI has enough data to recognize patterns in different topics and subjects, it can do those things much more efficiently, as well as in much lower time while also potentially working 24/7. While human interruption and oversight will always be required for AI based tasks, the number of people required will reduce drastically as time goes on.

The energy and environmental impacts are greater than we think.

The energy requirements for large scale AI, i.e. mass market, constant performance of complex AI tasks will become harder. Companies are advocating for nuclear energy as a potential solution to fuel AI's high energy demands. However, the process of passing bills and constructing these energy sources might be time-consuming, unless countries prioritize this matter. Even in those circumstances, the process of building it can be intricate and time-consuming. Furthermore, the considerable amount of water needed should not be forgotten, given that water is a finite and indispensable resource for the survival of the human race.

For reference: Microsoft reported a 30% increase in emissions from last year, just because of the resources required to run 'AI'.

Diversifying our skills faster than we are used to, will be crucial in adapting to the unpredictable times ahead. Because this time, we will be constantly competing against machines, for next two decades at least. I think in the next 8 years, possibly even within 5, there will be a global stabilization as the advancements in AI technology reach a point where they become stagnant. This will occur until the necessary infrastructure is upgraded worldwide to support complex tasks and the energy demands that come with them.

This period of stagnation will provide a much-needed opportunity for workers seeking to acquire new skills and individuals preparing themselves for the upcoming wave of rapid change. There are various potential pitfalls, including the possibility of stagnation prompting organizations to downsize, halt recruitment, or engage in short-term hiring bursts. Nonetheless, if AI remains stagnant, it indicates that individuals hired within the previous 5-7 years will have a greater chance of retaining their employment, since the uninterrupted flow of company operations is imperative. In any case, it is highly important to learn new skills to stay competitive in a job market influenced by AI.
And as I mentioned earlier, a lot of new jobs will come along while older ones fade away. All we need to do is keep up with the fast-paced change in the current market. It's changing faster than ever, and since AI has the ability to adapt and learn, it is something we might have to keep competing against for a long time.

There are a lot more things that can happen in the coming years, things which I didn't mention and changes that will come out of the blue. The future, like it always has been, will remain uncertain. The best we can do is learn, make calculated predictions to adapt as much as possible, and prepare for it.

CHAPTER FOUR

CONSUMERS AND BUSINESSES: LIKE WATER AND OIL

Our personal lives will be significantly affected by the widespread adoption of AI, more so than any other aspect, since our personal experiences make up the majority of our life; interacting with our environment and people, choosing hobbies, topics of interests, having discussions, and whatnot. The choices we make will be altered, the content we consume; social media and entertainment, things we buy or rent, news media, and trending topics of discussions, almost everything in our life will change as AI becomes more accurate and personalized. In this chapter, I'll dive into the impact of AI on various aspects of our daily lives, exploring its influence on work, communication, and even leisure activities.

Starting with...Buying habits.

By now, we're all used to seeing suggestions on Amazon(or any other e-commerce) for recommended products based on our search history, ads on YouTube for products that we might have searched for on google, or ads on any social media platform based either on our internet history or even from our conversations in real life. Yet, these suggestions still fall short of being truly accurate for most people. But no need to fret, within a span of 7 years or fewer, these suggestions will become so spot-on that you'll

question if the website can read your thoughts.
Current recommendations are, for the most part, based on:

- Age.
- Demographics.
- Keywords from your conversations in real life.
- Your internet search history and browser cookies.

In the future, the recommendations will track a multitude of metrics that were previously disregarded or not possible.

Such as:

- User's intentions and motivation behind the search of products and services.
- It will try to predict user emotions as well as the context behind the search.
- Based on your search history and cookies of other websites, it will try to predict product recommendations more accurately even before you type or search for them.
- AI can be used to accurately track users facial expressions and eye contact during ads and browsing via webcam and mic, and then recommend you products on which you maintain eye contact for longer.
- Let's say you're well into an eco-system of a company. You're browsing a shopping website on your PC, your watch from the same brand can sync your health metrics to recommend you products, while the PC tracks your eye movement to further enhance the recommendations. It could also sync data from your phone with your PC data, and use those to 'enhance' your shopping experience. (if they're both from the same company)

By leveraging hardware on phones, wearables, and computers, AI can track and aggregate data from various devices, resulting in highly accurate personalized recommendations for all users.

Lets take some different scenarios that will be possible in the coming

years:

1. You browse a few different phones on google that you're curious about. While you're browsing all the different options, the camera tracks your facial expression and eye movement. The algorithm, AI, then tries to predict the products you're disinterested in and the products that you looked at for longer than a few seconds; the products you might be interested in. With the help of the neural network and algorithms, it can then filter out recommendations and personalize your e-commerce experience, since almost every major online store uses google API today. It's the same for laptops and PC's with IR camera, they can track your eye movement very accurately, even more than just a camera, and then *monitor* your expressions and body language.

2. Imagine you're in your car with some friends, going to watch avatar 4 in 2029, and your phone is with you. The mic will then listen to all your conversations and use speech & voice recognition to identify your interests, preferences, hobbies, habits, relationship status, gender, etc. If you talk about buying new headphones, the mic will pick it up and give you headphone recommendations when you open your phone or an app. Oh wait, its not just the phone, the infotainment system in your car, with its own mic will also track your speech and send it to the car company for AI training, showing relevant ads into the car navigation and maps, and other secret reasons like selling it ;)

3. It's not limited to just phones and PCs though, our health and location data are tracked by wearables such as smartwatches, smart-rings, and smart-glasses. These wearables can track your lifestyle habits, travel habits/locations, your health condition and medications, which is then synced with the cloud server. Your data is then used by companies to feed to its algorithms for personalized recommendations on how to improve your physical & mental health, lifestyle, and overall wellness. Which is very useful, given the increasing costs of doctor visits, BUT.. it doesn't end there. You could also get personalized recommendation for doctors or hospitals, based on who paid to be on top, just like how you have to pay to be higher on top in search engines.(not right now, but this has a very high chance of happening, based on the trends. Unless the government steps in to regulate, which can take over 50 years zzz...)

The grey area of modern laws.

There are numerous conditions listed on each app and for each feature within it; about how companies collect and use our data, but who has time to read such a long list of terms & conditions, we are all very busy people. And don't for even a minute think companies are unaware of it, it is completely intentional, because companies know that most of us don't read tens and hundreds of pages for every feature and app we use and download. Making the list as long as possible, while also keeping it vague by distributing a simple condition across multiple bullet points is how they create legal loopholes.

Businesses all around the world are rapidly pushing AI technologies, and one of the main motivations for their aggressive approach is because they know that governments tend to take a significant amount of time to pass regulations and laws for new technologies. They want to get as many people as possible to be dependent on AI. So when the laws are actually being passed, these organizations get to lobbying and the government is compelled to accept the terms set by these organizations for new regulations.

I mean, just look at the "**AI oversight board**" that the US government has formed. It consists of CEO's from Nvidia, Google, IBM, Adobe, Microsoft, AWS, AMD, and Cisco. If anyone benefits from a global AI push, more than anyone, it's these companies. And they are the ones who will make major decisions about implementation of AI by the government, into every aspect of our lives. Surely they will think of what's best for the environment, consumers, and a sustainable future where resources are not scarce, instead of creating regulations that will benefit their trillion dollar organizations in their quarterly and yearly reports.

According to multiple researches, the average reading time of an entire terms & conditions document is 90-120 minutes.

And with the introduction of AI, cloud services, and data protection laws changing, this list is going to potentially become even longer in the future. This is why some companies are found to be abusing loopholes and consumer protection laws, decades after a product launch. But it is what it is, as consumers we can't do much to change these business practices, BUT what we can do is be more conscious of these practices and choose our purchases accordingly.

The best way to influence brands and their business practices; our wallets. Pressure caused by declining sales compels companies to be more transparent and ethical, or take some radical steps and dig their own grave.

Nothing gives CEO's more panic than seeing red on the sales and revenue charts. The fear of missing out on the quarterly and yearly bonuses can give them sleepless nights. It's the same reason we see mass layoffs; when CEO's fail to make any meaningful improvements to their business, the easier option is to fire employees and make up for the losses, and putting the blame on 'AI' in official reports to avoid taking accountability for their short-sighted leadership and unpreparedness for adapting to newer technologies.

This approach works when seeing results in reports, and in finances, but is detrimental for any organization in the long-term, if constantly repeated, especially towards its reputation and public perception.

While we're on the topic of loopholes, there's another major shift in the industry tagging along. That is, yes you guessed it right, software and subscriptions. Its no coincidence that all major tech companies today are focusing on connected technologies and apps. Now that millions of devices are already in circulation and customers are holding onto their devices for longer, the industry needs to find a new cash cow. The answer to that was, tighter control over the software in these millions of devices, as well as paid services to access exclusive apps and features for a constant(and consistent) subscription price.

The advancements in hardware have slowed down in recent years, especially compared to the rapid upgrades seen in the 2000s or even until 2018. The direct consequence of companies' unceasing pursuit of hardware growth is the industry-wide adoption of long-term software support and app-based subscriptions, even in products that might get little to no benefit from it.

Since hardware is almost always a long-term purchase, companies cannot sell you anything more until you upgrade to a newer model after 3-7 years. Even if a company is not declining but stagnant, they look to diversify and offer new products & services in a bid to increase revenue. Uniform profits are also considered problematic for companies that are constantly seeking to increase their sales and stock value. Especially the extreme capitalist ones, that only care about short term quarterly revenue and disregard moral and ethical exploitations.

Subscriptions are good?

To a lot of extent, long-term software support is good for customers. We get reassurance that the hardware we are buying will be supported and improved constantly for many years to come. On the flip side, it creates a new avenue for companies to continually modify or remove features over the course of those years, with the purpose of promoting their subscription services and other products within their ecosystem.

Subscription models or cloud-based versions with subscription have become the norm for almost all major products today. Subscriptions offer the temptation of regular updates and new 'AI' features, but they also mean you'll be paying for the software indefinitely without ever truly owning it. While the core idea is sound, the way it is executed can vary. This becomes even more noticeable when an unscrupulous company withdraws product licenses from users' devices for minor reasons, effectively banning them from using the app they paid for as well as possibly locking them out of years of worth of personal data.

Companies, in their pursuit of individuality, aim to differentiate their products by making them exclusive and unique, rather than conforming to a global standard. Here are some issues that it can cause:

- Established companies offer free features, strategically wait until a substantial portion of their customer base becomes dependent on them, and then gradually raise prices and introduce higher-priced tiers. Once this happens, most customers would have already become accustomed to the specific service and its cloud offerings, making it more challenging to switch. Especially because now all their habits and data are dependant on that app.

- Inconsistent file compatibility is another common issue found in similar products from different brands. For example: Microsoft word is the most widely used productivity software, but there are many others with their own version of word and offer their own set of features. Many users use different default extensions, and this can lead to problems with formatting and compatibility when you convert and send your files to someone using a different office suite.

- Again, features can be moved from one subscription tier to another and we're at the mercy of a company. Let's say there's a feature that almost everyone uses in an app. The company can then move that feature to a more expensive subscription tier, rather than keep it where it always has been. Forcing people to either upgrade or give up on the feature that they love.

- Merge different products into one and increase the prices by a considerate 10% or so. To give you some perspective, I'll share a hypothetical situation: Let's assume a company has three products: x, y, z. In order to address the low sales of z, the company has made the decision to merge it with y into a single software product. Next, they promote the features of Z as a key component of Y's latest 'major' update, raising the subscription price and launching promotional campaigns to highlight the significant changes. Even though none of these features are new. And although it isn't necessarily bad, it's unfortunate that even those who don't require these new features are compelled to pay the increased cost because of reduced choices of products by the company, leaving users with no alternative.

- And this happens because once companies realize that you're used to one of their products, they know many will hesitate to move all their data to a new service and go through all the hassle. Thus, organizations increase cost slowly, lets say by 10% every year for 3 years. In this way, every year the customer thinks "oh, its just 10% increase, I can afford it".

You would own nothing, no matter how much you pay...

There are countless other approaches to integrating subscriptions. Companies commonly explore unique methods to introduce additional revenue streams into their products, but they ultimately discard most of these ideas after the initial testing phase and never bring them to public knowledge. For example: John Riccitiello, former CEO of EA, said that players in shooting games can be charged to reload weapons each time. Another idea in gaming that Rockstar considered with the announcement of GTA 6: Charging players based on time played. So, the longer you want to play, the more you'll have to pay. Rockstar dismissed that they are not implementing this in the game, but that leak was more than likely to test public reaction.

On the other hand, GM removing android auto and apple carplay; they will instead sell their own software services and features, restrict the ecosystem to only what they provide and reduce the choices for customers. Implementing this strategy enables the company to exert increased control over both the vehicle and the data it gathers, including tighter control over subscription services.

Another major shift that happened recently; Adobe changing it's terms, that they will use your personal work to train their AI. Regardless if you're making something for a business, or for personal use, the rightful ownership of your content will be shared between you and adobe to use it as they like.

Companies face a greater challenge in implementing new paid services rather than simply creating them. Customers tend to be cautious when previously free features are suddenly included as paid options. Typically, companies have to introduce new features in order to entice potential customers to buy their subscription services. However, even with these enhancements, there is always a possibility of negative publicity for the brand.

In contrast to the GM example; BMW implemented similar features. They locked apple carplay for $80/year and heated seats were locked behind a subscription as well. Eventually, both of these subscription services had to be discontinued and the features made available for free. This was in response to a strong negative reaction to paid subscriptions, which was witnessed in nearly every major global market where BMW operates.

It's a free market, or is it...?

Well, it's a free market and no one can force companies to follow similar revenue models. The availability of an open ecosystem that can adapt to various customer needs is what really matters. By not allowing android auto and apple carplay, GM could prevent customers from accessing features that could easily be done from their phones, forcing them to wait for GM to incorporate features into their car's infotainment system.

But the biggest issue is; In order to control the market, big companies deliberately decrease the supply by acquiring and shutting down smaller businesses in their industry. Then they raise prices to capitalize on the artificial "higher demand".

With AI at the helm, companies can use large amounts of customer data that they have, and generate new monetization models based around customer habits and reluctance. Even without AI, humans have been following these practices, but they take much longer and humans have personal bias and morality when making these decisions, which can be good or bad, depending on who is making these decisions.

Lower human involvement means less emotions and morals involved in decision making, which in turn means morals and ethics are tossed away completely.

AI's lack of emotions, ethical thoughts, or morality makes it even more terrifying in the wrong hands.

Imagine a morally corrupt leader, his heart devoid of empathy, ruthlessly orchestrating the massacre of thousands who dare to challenge his authority. The leaders' followers, if they have a sense of morality and recognize the injustice, will attempt to obstruct his plans or abstain from executing his orders. However, if his soldiers were replaced with robots, he could easily manipulate them through a computer command, and they would ruthlessly exterminate all those people.

Governments and independent organizations should enforce strict regulations on that particular aspect of AI, in order to prevent it from becoming a potential threat. Yet, the sad reality is that the promise of monetary profit can make people submit themselves willingly and abandon their moral compass, a constant theme throughout the history of mankind.

AI can be utilized for more than just taking lives; it has the power to manipulate the masses by disseminating propaganda via different sources and formats. The combination of these factors, along with the growing power of social media, can lead to lasting repercussions.

I expect consumerism to be on a gradual increase in the next 7 years and stabilizing somewhere around 2034, if there are no major global wars or events like covid-19. The transition and adoption into AI and AI-based products will empower companies, governments, and influential individuals to exert greater control over the information accessible to the masses.

Human communication will see a major shift

Speaking of consumerism, there is another significant factor that influences purchasing trends: human communication. The way people talk to each other, behave, take actions, and think, will all change drastically with the adoption and improvements in AI. Today's generation exhibits drastically different social habits compared to the previous one, largely influenced by technology, especially social media.
The increasing popularity of AI-based smart wearables and advancements in online communication have opened up many possibilities that could play out in the future.

- One of the most thoroughly researched concepts is the effect of increased isolation on our brain. The rapid progress of technology will bring forth a new era where smart-glasses and other wearables will enable us to communicate with others effortlessly, regardless of physical distance. Poor emotional and mental development is more likely to occur, especially in children and teenagers, impacting their brain development. Up until the age of 25, our brain continues to mature, and it heavily relies on consistent exposure to social groups, knowledge acquisition, physical touch, and exposure to diverse opinions from people of various backgrounds. Neglecting these factors can disrupt our overall development.Physical contact with humans, such as the gentle touch of a handshake or the warm embrace of a hug, plays a vital role in training and stimulating our brain's reward system. It is also a proven method to increase the likelihood of a long-term relationship with people, as it taps into the natural human instinct of wanting to feel close to others.

- This is why so many people do a hug or handshake when they meet:
  - Physical sensations like handshakes and hugs are proven to improve trust, affection and empathy between people.
  - Hugs have also been proven to release dopamine and serotonin, especially in children and socially isolated adults. This helps in mood improvement and emotional regulation.
  - The release of hormones not only help our mood, but it also enhances our body and improves our productivity while also making us more emotionally stable.
  - Gut regulates most of our hormones and a healthy balance of them improves our digestion as well as immune system.
  - Our brain also remembers the intimate touch sensations for a much longer time than virtual conversations. When that touch sensation is stored as a memory, it is directly associated with the emotional response of happy or pleasant.

- Insufficient social interaction in our early years can have a detrimental impact on brain development later in life. Engaging in conversations with a diverse range of individuals, observing their body language and emotional reactions, plays a crucial role in enhancing our social skills, regulating our emotions, and recognizing behavioral patterns.

- Public places filled with people, noise, and voices are particularly important for children under the age of 8, as they need constant and regular exposure to such environments. When they don't receive enough exposure, they are at a higher risk of developing mental health issues like anxiety as they age, or developing socially isolating habits to make up for the lack of social interaction in their lives. The older we become, the more rigid our brain's ability to adapt becomes. Thus, exposing children to a dynamic environment is a key factor in ensuring their ability to adapt and succeed in the global society as adults goes smoothly.

- Personal boundaries with different people, such as friends, family, and partners, start to become blurry online. Anyone can access your social media details and posts, regardless if you want to share that information with them or not. Social media's impact on personal boundaries can be problematic, as blocking someone on a platform can potentially strain relationships if they interpret it as a personal affront. Therefore, socially interacting with a variety of individuals, we learn to set personal boundaries in more productive and effective ways. Again, this is technically a part of adaptability.

The integration of AI is expected to further enhance our online experience, leading to increased global adoption of these habits. This will especially be evident with the rise in adoption of VR/AR products, and customizable AI personalities such as some companies are offering "AI friends and partners", which will rather promote another reason for men/women seeking relationships, to stay away from social interactions. I'm not blaming these people, but when someone has social anxiety and instead of them getting motivated and uplifted by the society, they are given more reasons to isolate, it can push them further down the rabbit hole. Since you can customize your AI "partner's" personality to validate your thoughts and fantasies, you might feel more accepted and satisfied by talking to it, rather than talking to people in real life who all have different opinions and may not agree with you on everything.

This isn't as big of an issue right now, but in the future, as AI gets better at predicting your thoughts and feelings, it could cause more problems for vulnerable people. Without proper oversight, AI has the potential to sway people's behavior by validating their thoughts and false beliefs, leading to both positive and negative consequences. And it could be deployed in everyday products such as phones and social media websites.

BUT,

On the other hand, it can also bring about positive effects on both individuals and society as a whole, as it has the potential to significantly enhance communication, increase awareness, and increase education accessibility for the masses.

How we choose to implement AI on a large scale will determine whether it becomes a savior or a threat. It could be used to:

- For individuals feeling lonely, having an AI friend can be highly beneficial as it gradually motivates them to make positive changes in their lives by offering a range of suggestions, reminders, and tips, similar to a therapist but at a fraction of the cost. By examining the conversation history of each user, these 'AI' suggestions would take into account their emotions, experiences, and intentions. By involving doctors and using medical data, the AI model could be trained to be more ethical and accurate, presenting a wide range of possibilities for helping millions around the world.

- A major obstacle would involve designing an AI model that doesn't cause negative emotional responses in users, particularly those with mental health conditions who may be more vulnerable to feelings of criticism or being attacked. This challenge is especially prominent when considering individuals with PTSD, as preventing any triggers of negative emotions would pose a significant difficulty due to the nature of it.

- How about a real time AI teacher? It can teach individual users' various social and communication skills. This can be done via a VR/AR headset, in which the headset can use AI features and sensors to track eye and body movement, and your voice. It can then use the data to compare it with different models, and offer you practical tips for self-improvement while also giving instructions on how to put those tips into practice. In fact, it can demonstrate how to do things correctly right in the glasses in real time, and you can then practice, just like you would with a teacher in front of you.

- Positive reinforcement, motivation, non-judgemental replies, and 24/7 availability are some things that make AI a great learning platform. While human intervention remains essential, AI can offer a safe space for feedback-seeking individuals, free from judgment.

- While it may be challenging, the primary task is to avoid people from becoming excessively dependent on AI, especially since individuals with mental health issues often seek a source of dependency. The goal should always be to make sure that individuals gradually learn to be independent, and use the service as a platform to learn and grow at different stages of life. This will enable the society to have smarter and more productive people, thus improving the overall state of a country.

Although that might be a little tough for companies that care more about profits than their positive impact on people.

I believe the roll-out of AI-based personalities and people-centered approach is a powerful force that can bring about significant positive change in society and individuals across the globe. However, there are downsides to it, and companies often prioritize consumerism over educating customers about technologies.
Instead of empowering customers to make independent decisions, this gives businesses the ability to mold customer opinions.

Companies employ a clever tactic of positioning, advertising, and recommending their products and services to potential customers, even if they acknowledge that these offerings may not completely satisfy the customer's requirements. The goal is to maximize sales by providing multiple products or services that together fulfill a specific customer need, rather than selling just one service that can fulfill multiple needs.

To quote a famous saying on the internet "**create a problem, then sell a solution**".

It's what some people like to call 'customer perception'.

Every company dreams of influencing customer perception and opinion, but Apple stands out as one of the few that has achieved this feat exceptionally well. The human-centric approach to AI is a widely recognized concept that highlights the significance of taking into account human emotions, behavior, and well-being during the development and deployment of AI models/products on a large scale.
The complicated part is to find a way for humanity and technology to coexist harmoniously, as the advancement of AI has the potential to exponentially enhance its intelligence and self-awareness once it surpasses a certain level of development. Moreover, there are multiple potential challenges that may arise with implementation and mass adoption of these technologies.

Issues such as: Ethical and moral responsibilities, privacy concerns, job displacement, increased discrimination, polarization, existential crisis, and lower control of people over decision making towards the future of the country and society i.e. politics.

In today's digital age, people are spending more time online than ever before. They are actively engaging with others through social media platforms, sharing significant aspects of their lives, connecting with people from different corners of the globe, and keeping up with the updates of those they follow. A pretty significant amount of population is consuming news via social media completely, giving up on traditional news media in record numbers.

Take TikTok, for example, which has witnessed unparalleled growth as a social media giant. It achieved over 650 million users in its first year, 2016, and by the end of 2023, its active user count had exceeded a billion. There is a smooth projected growth in the number of users, and it is anticipated to become the top social media platform worldwide, unless there are potential bans in the US and Europe. The population density in developing countries contributes to a much larger pool of potential social media users, even if the actual rate of adoption is not as high as initially projected. Compared to other social media platforms, TikTok's algorithm is highly effective in keeping users engaged with recommended content, leading to longer periods of time spent on the app. Albeit their legal cases, TikTok stands out among other apps by effectively utilizing AI's capabilities and implementing user psychology methods, resulting in a superior business model.

The advancements in social media will be a goldmine for advertisers, as well as for celebrities and politicians. Their platform provides a valuable opportunity for businesses and individuals to advertise and increase their visibility, especially since TikTok's user base consists primarily of individuals under 30. A primarily youthful audience enables companies and politicians to reach the new generation on a much bigger scale than traditional media.

Growth of AI will only make it more influential

With generative AI improving rapidly in the last 3 years, social media will see larger amounts of interaction and increased usage by the amount of time spent.

For instance, with the advancements in generative AI, social media platforms will be able to generate highly realistic and personalized content for users. This could include AI-generated posts, comments, and even entire conversations that mimic human behavior, for the memes of course. As a result, users will be more engaged on social media, because the content will be more relevant, entertaining, and tailored to their preferences.

AI and its subsequent technologies have the potential to reshape the world as we know it, heralding a new era where society operates on a global scale, marking a monumental chapter in the history of humanity. The negative and positive changes brought about by this 'AI generation' will undoubtedly be remembered for centuries to come, unless someone destroys the entire planet, marking it as the pivotal moment where everything began.

Selective personalisation can go awry in the long-term...

The internet has made global connectivity and communication almost instant, allowing people from different cultures, races, and religions to easily share their opinions on any topic. However, these discussions can quickly turn contentious. And the solution that social media companies came up with, was, adding topic filters and using algorithms to show you content similar to what you engage with. Instead, this caused online communities to become more divided, ultimately leading to an escalation of conflicts and increased polarization.

You know how kids in school make groups, are not particularly friendly to other groups, and occasionally fight with other groups? Well, it's the same thing on social media now, but on a much larger and global scale, and now adults are taking part in online fights, along with kids. These events unfolded on a significantly larger scale during recent elections worldwide, and the pandemic. Even with the recent wars, a large amount of online polarization and fake content is being spread.

The effects of these changes online will trickle down slowly into our everyday lives, via changes in thoughts and behavior of not just us but the people around us as well. That's why it's crucial to talk about the moral and ethical side of AI, so we can keep hostility and polarization in check.

Time will tell how things play out, whether companies take the moral high ground and do what is better for humanity, if they'll be forced to change by governments, or if the governments and organizations work together to manipulate people.

IT'S USE OR BE USED: CAN WE CO-EXIST?

In this chapter I'll be talking about how we can use AI in different parts of our thinking and action patterns, in order to improve them. To change the basics of how we think, and look at things with a fresh perspective, is the first step if we want to change anything in our lives. So, let's begin.

At this point, widespread integration and adoption of AI and AI based technologies is inevitable. AI will come in all shapes and sizes, metaphorically, in the form of connected-infrastructure, products, and services that we might need to use occasionally in our lives, if not every day. That is why, taking advantage of AI to progress in both personal and professional life becomes ever so important.

However, in order to fully exploit the advantages of this rapidly evolving technology, it is becoming more crucial to understand its fundamentals, rather than just the product features. If you're wondering "are the basics really more important than knowing the features?", well, they both are technically.

"Ignorance is bliss" is a quote that can be really helpful in many scenarios, but not here, because AI will eventually become impossible to ignore. And not knowing about it would rather just reduce your potential growth opportunities not only in your profession but also as a human being.

AI is an add-on, not replacement!

It is crucial to continually update and adapt one's skills and knowledge throughout life. Without staying up-to-date with the latest advancements and developments, people may struggle to keep up with rapid changes in all aspects of life. Therefore, continuous learning and development are essential. Once you have a solid foundation and understanding of the basics, it becomes easier to comprehend and adapt to future changes.

Learning the basics is a short-term intensive effort, for the ease of adapting for years to come.

Continuous learning ensures that you are equipped with the necessary knowledge and expertise to thrive in a rapidly evolving technological landscape.

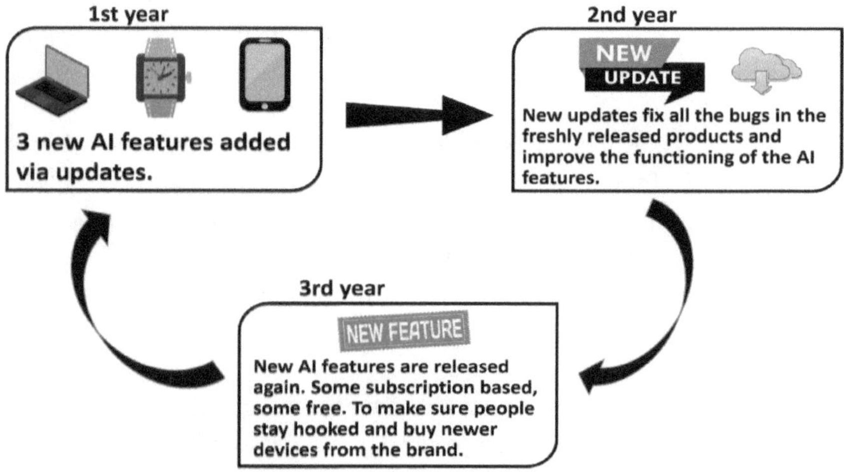

The 3 year cycle

Currently these changes happen, on average, every 2 years. Where the first year is implementation of new features and second year is used to work on polishing those features. In the third year, however, companies yet again introduce new AI features and repeat the two-year cycle of updating those features. This fast roll-out of features is happening because the global competition today is so cutthroat that no one wants to be left behind and everyone wants to gain the first mover advantage.

Tech industry, especially consumer tech, has one of the lowest brand loyalty across all consumer industries. Apple being the exception. On the other hand, for professionals, implementation of new technologies and practices throughout the entire business model within a company are happening at the fastest rate ever.

The demands of skills across industries are changing rapidly. To accommodate for these fast changes, can be quite problematic; for both employees and companies. Constant resource shuffling not only increases costs and delays in delivering promised results, but it also takes a toll on the performance and emotional stability of employees. Seeing this volatile and parlous environment, most companies are now playing it safe by slowly reducing their hiring, laying off employees, and streamlining automation across departments.

Once the ground settles, companies will again hire en masse with requirements for the new and 'modern' skills. Today it's AI that's causing disruption, by 2040 it will be the beginning of the 'age of robots' and seamless wearables. Robotics will be in a similar spot as AI is today; just starting to roll out in the mainstream consumer market and in the job market, demands for newer skills in the industry will keep on evolving, while older skills will slowly become irrelevant, perhaps not as drastic as today since AI, ML, and NLP are major parts of the robotics industry. The AI of the future will undergo extensive changes and be far more complex than it is now.

Whenever a groundbreaking technology emerges, it is embraced globally, regardless of the country, industry, or economy. It doesn't always have to be consumer market, industry processes such as logistics, supply chain, manufacturing, even the military and space organizations benefit from it. But that's just how technology is. Once the base is near perfect, there are thousand of different ways to build things on it and everyone in the industry will have their own differentiating vision as to how the technology should be used. Over time, these varying implementations lead to newer ideas and birth of new technologies.

<u>Where we are today...</u>

Here we are today, seeing the rise of AI with our very own eyes. So buckle up, because we are witnessing a technological revolution happening right in front of us, and it's going to be cruising at an unfathomable speed into a myriad number of paths.

Let's start with, perhaps, the part of our lives where AI has the most influence, i.e. our daily life.

Leveraging technology in our everyday life is the most important chore that subconsciously influences every aspect of our life and its future potential, mainly in the form of thoughts and actions. Today, there are:

- Smart lights.
- Smart speakers with AI assistant connected to other smart gadgets; to form a cohesive eco-system.
- Smart phones with both cloud based and on-device AI.
- PC's with unlimited potential for AI based apps and features, scaling with hardware advancements in the future.
- Wearables like smartwatches, bands, rings, glasses etc.
- Smart-TV's, washing machines, Air-conditioners, automated vacuum cleaner bots and other appliances.

Well, when we have so many smart objects around us, why not use them to their potential? Rather than only using them in the traditional sense of an appliance. Our brain is a majestic entity. Unlike AI, our brain possesses an incredible cognitive capacity to function effortlessly and carry out tasks with exceptional efficiency*
***With consistent exposure to knowledge and training of course.**

It will take several decades for AI to reach even 50% of a human because of the brain's complex structure. The strength of the brain is not just about solving equations or problems, but about its ability to be conscious, be independent, have emotions, morals, and ethics. On top of that, we can constantly learn and change throughout our lives based on our experience, so the brain never stops evolving until we die :(

While our goal is to develop conscious AI that matches or surpasses human intelligence, it will likely take several decades to achieve this, and there will still be numerous imperfections and inaccuracies because human mind's strength is in its ability to be conscious and have emotions, and not just be logical. Theory of mind, as I mentioned in the first chapter, is a proof of that.

Given the intelligence and efficiency of AI, why not leverage it to increase productivity and further enhance your own capabilities? By automating the boring and monotonous daily tasks, we can use the saved mental and emotional capacity towards more productive tasks. Imagine we can save enough time to sleep for those extra 5 minutes in the morning.

That's exactly what we are going to do.

Traveling, cooking, cleaning, and leisure activities in our personal lives will undergo significant changes, either positive or negative, depending on your perspective. If you have any smart-appliance at home, you can use the smart features to setup a routine and the machine will act on its own and repeat the pattern everyday. You don't need to go back and perform the same boring actions on them everyday.

Let's take the example that I mentioned in the introduction; I have a smart speaker, connected with my smart-lights, smart-refrigerator, washing machine, and TV. Now, with just my smart-speakers, I can give commands to control each of these devices, without being physically present in-front of them and they will execute actions on their own. If you're someone like me, who doesn't like using voice commands, you're in luck because you can do all these things via your phone acting as the central remote for almost all the appliances and devices that you own.

1. By leveraging these smart and 'AI' features, we can not only save time but also save a lot of frustration. All these features can be used to remove redundancy from our daily routine, and make the flow between different activities seamless, without having to stop for each task. As for the naysayers, people are not getting lazier because of technology. People are getting lazier because they are not replacing their habits with new ones. Over time, **this dependency on automated tasks may hinder our ability**

to think critically and problem-solve independently.

When technology automates tasks, it does so with the intent for streamlining repetitive and mundane tasks, freeing up time and resources for individuals to focus on more creative and innovative endeavors . But some people might, instead of replacing their routine with new tasks, just spend time on leisure activities and hence can be seen as becoming lazy due to technology. **For instance:** If smart appliances do the daily cleaning & washing tasks for me, I can then use that time to learn a new skill. If I just sit back, do nothing, because the machine is doing my old tasks, I would be rather unproductive and lazy. In the saved time, I could do a new course or learn a new skill, well surely not in just a few days, but over the period of several months, depending on what it is that I want to learn.
We all have our chains weighing us down, whether they're financial, time-related, emotional, personal relationships, mental/physical illness, or something else. However, when we utilize technology to automate certain aspects of our lives, it's important to track and allocate the time saved towards new knowledge and skills. Without tracking our time consumption, it becomes hard to juggle everyday tasks. I mean, some people are naturally and effortlessly good at resource management, while most of us require some form of time and resource tracking. Just like most of us track our finances, I hope so, we should track the most important resource in this planet; the unstoppable ticking time, that stops for no one.

This shift towards automation not only improves productivity but also encourages continuous learning and growth. **When our brain is consistently stimulated and encouraged to think**, it becomes more adept at regulating our thoughts and emotions, on top of the new information that we're learning.

2. The advancements in modern chips have made wearables the biggest benefactor, and their performance will continue to increase. One of the greatest benefits of wearables and AI is the increased emphasis on health and fitness, especially among the mass population. Making health monitoring not only more accessible but also more affordable.

If someone had told us in 2001 that we would have the ability to monitor our heart rate, ECG, SPO2, and even blood sugar levels(coming soon) directly from a watch, without having to buy specialized devices or going to the hospital, we would have found it hard to believe. Before 2030, we will have accurate blood glucose level monitoring in our watches. There are ongoing considerations for research and development in features, such as emotion detection for mental health improvements, sweat monitoring, and body fat level measurement. I am 99% sure we will have those eventually, but when is the biggest question? I predict 99% accurate sensors by 2035. I'm also very certain we will have early cancer detection thanks to chip implants, but that might take much longer than 2035.

With all these features fitting right into a small device that you can wear on your wrist or body, it's a no-brainer to use them. Undetected and subtle changes in our body, especially for people with underlying health conditions, are impossible for us to detect on our own. There have been countless cases of people being saved due to early detection of irregularities in heart rate as well as by fall detection; a feature that calls emergency services if you become unconscious by either suddenly falling or if you've been in an accident.

Hypothetically, there is less than a 5% chance of something like that happening, but that 5% could prove fatal if there are delays in getting medical help.

With each new feature that is introduced, the difficulty of using these products grows as we postpone using wearables, resulting in feeling overwhelmed when we actually do try to use these smart products. That is why adopting these awesome gadgets right now is the best time. Adopting them today will be ensure smooth transition into the next generation of wearables. (that is less than 5 years away)

3. With the help of AI, robotics, and other AI-based wearables, socializing will reach new levels of immersion, benefiting companies and people alike. Shops/Offices will have holograms, transparent displays, connected technologies that transfer catalog directly to your phone/smart glasses, restaurants can display their menu instantly, as well as give customers an accurate image of food portions and nutritional information via immersive 3D images. This seamless experience allows you to effortlessly checkout from shops, complete instant payments using your wearable accessory as you walk out.

Just imagine a situation where you can seamlessly drive your car without the need to stop for refueling, effortlessly enter social events without ticket/pass checks, and shop without interruptions for items or payments. The purpose of technology in these scenarios is to eliminate queues and other hiccups, thus providing a seamless transition of activities in your life. With technology, you can carry on with your daily routine while it handles all the bothersome and time-consuming tasks that would have typically demanded your focus. These are just a few examples of what the future could look like, of course these are varying and might change eventually, based on public acceptance/response.

These instances are just the tip of iceberg, a large part of our lives will be automated by AI. Thus, replacing our old habits with new ones will be crucial. Automation is only bad when we fail to evolve as an individual and let technology take charge of our life.

4. Beyond video calls and texting, our relationships with people and the way we communicate will see drastic changes. Using VR, AR, and MR for video calls will be possible, rather than just looking at your screen. Meeting new people, and making friends will become easier with the adoption of these technologies. You can meet someone via VR and have a visual meeting online, before meeting them for the first time. This helps a lot in filtering out people, that could make fake profiles via text/video, although hacking VR to display false images will be possible anyways, but for most people that might be too hard to do.
We'll also have instant translation and be able to talk to people globally without needing to know the language, although we somewhat have real-time translation right now, it is not very accurate and timely.

5. Certain wearables will be able to use your health monitoring data to consider your emotional and physical condition and give suggestions on how to reply to texts, emails and even conversation happening in real time. The benefits are not limited to just these activities, for people with disabilities it could open so many options that were not possible before. They can immerse themselves in shopping via holograms and projectors, check the different sizes and fittings without going to the store. They can attend concerts and events, by using VR/MR and get the experience of being present there physically.

They can meet tons of people via VR and talk to them as you would in real life, there are also devices being made to act as stimulants for physical contact and even being able to taste the food you see online, although i doubt that device will ever get out of the niche category, and be probably used for a lot of other purposes than what it was intended for. But yes, technology holds potential to assist almost everyone, if used correctly, and we should use it to its full capabilities to upgrade our mind and body.

Trends and habits will change much faster with the rapid change in technologies, we need to make sure we are not left behind.

6. By leveraging technology, sports and hobbies can be enhanced through the use of performance tracking and personalized recommendations for improving movement, techniques, and other key aspects of the activity. The use of body trackers opens up the possibility of utilizing synced health data from other wearables to recommend personalized diet and rest schedules. For example, in the context of football, recommendations can be provided on various angles to position your leg before kicking the ball or on different movement patterns required to successfully reach the ball. By incorporating chips into shoes, helmets, balls, and other accessories, as well as equipment like rackets and sticks, you can monitor your performance. The data collected can then be used to track your movements and performance, providing valuable insights to enhance your future games.
By incorporating technology into the seats and audience section, such as large holograms, vibration motors for a 4DX like experience, and streaming to VR/AR glasses, the audience can enjoy an immersive experience and stay connected with real-time updates, statistics, and interactive features, ensuring they don't miss any action despite being seated far away.

What exactly is self-improvement...?

We can use ChatGPT and Gemini to upgrade our personal and social lives as well, just like we can for our professional lives. We've all heard about self-development, but what does it really mean when it's applied into the real world?

Well, the answer is subjective and varies from person to person, as everyone has their own interpretation and understanding of things. Our perspectives, experiences, and beliefs play a significant role in how we perceive and comprehend the world. What may appear logical and true to one individual could be seen as illogical and false to another. Those who argue otherwise fail to recognize and appreciate the distinct qualities of each person and instead make broad generalizations about large groups of individuals.

Let me give you a reference to back it up:

The practice of hiring personal teachers and skill development professionals for children is common among the wealthy. In older times, this practice was employed by the royal families. They would hire exclusive teachers who possessed unique knowledge and skill-sets to educate their children.
Each child has their own unique view of the world, including how they perceive people, how they think, and the way they learn. Understanding the individual needs of each person and tailoring the learning experience accordingly is a demanding task that cannot be physically or mentally accomplished by everyone. Personal teachers bridge that gap by dedicating all their energy to one or a few children, investing their time and effort to truly understand each individual. In contrast, in schools, the overwhelming number of students in each class, ranging from 30-50, renders it impractical for a teacher to attend to the needs of every individual student. As a result, numerous students feel neglected and turn to the internet for guidance or opt for private instructors.

In this way, AI can gradually narrow the divide by tailoring itself to individuals' unique understanding and interpretation of the world. Not all of us can afford personal teachers and professionals, but AI is more affordable for the masses. I mean, sure it lacks the empathy and emotional development that a human teacher would provide, but we'll reach there to a basic extent pretty soon, as technology advances. AI has the potential to offer a highly personalized learning experience for both children and adults, benefiting a wide range of individuals in their understanding of complex subjects that may not be effectively taught in traditional school or university settings, where teaching methods tend to be more generalized and accommodating to a larger number of students, neglecting individual development.

The beauty of us humans, and the entire humanity, is in our individuality and our ability to combine these unique skills of each person to achieve the unthinkable. When we generalize people, like in many institutions, we dismiss their unique qualities, diverse ideas, and individual interests, consequently blocking their potential for growth. That would be as if we had turned into robots, losing our uniqueness and conforming to a uniform set of behaviors and beliefs.

A good structure and method of education helps children prosper, not only helping them to learn but also helping them in realizing their potential and developing their abilities to strive in the future. And it's not just for people; A country that has a well-built and comprehensive system for nurturing their youth will not only prosper and grow, but also create a bright future for generations to come.
BUT, I cannot emphasize enough that AI based learning/teaching should be an add-on to real life, not replace it. Schools and universities hold immense value beyond just book knowledge, and they should never be ignored. For things such as social behavior, habits, and the ability to communicate with all kinds of people are just some of the skills that we learn in school.

However, a good environment and company within school, university, and even your professional environment will help you in utilizing your potential, regardless of your age. As for emotional development, it is something that would require the guidance of adults(for children), friends, family, and other professionals such as mental health therapists. More onto that later.

Now that you have an idea, let's get back to the question: what really is self-development?

It's pretty simple; self-development is improving our lives constantly for as long as we are alive. It's like buying new phones every 3-6 years, we upgrade to what's the latest technology or the trend. In the same way, our professional and personal skills need to be constantly upgraded as well, for

us to strive in this experience called life. Now, there are a lot of things that fall under self-development, things ranging from cognitive and psychological skills, to impulse and behavioral management, and everything in between.
Once we work on improving these aspects of our lives, it will improve everything included in our daily life i.e. stress management, emotional and logical response to people and situations, improvements in our skills to do things more effectively and efficiently, and improving our relationships.

The better we understand ourselves, the better we can help others. Just like when you go into an airplane, there are constant reminders "make sure to wear the masks on your face and stabilize your breathing, before helping others". Its because if we aren't physically or emotionally stable ourselves, we might make half-hearted attempts at helping others and not just harm ourselves but possibly make things worse for others with our approach. With that same thought of line is why militaries around the world have such rigorous training, it is to make sure that people in military are always on the best of their physical and mental health, in order to make decisions and act instantly to whatever situation may arise. While that kind of training is not needed for most people, but that is what we call self-development. We can develop and improve almost anything in life, but the approach for it is always unique to you, your personality, your emotions, and your behavior.

If you look at someone successful and try to copy their approach, it may not always work and you might not even get positive results, but that is not because you can't do things. It's because how your mind works is different from others, we all have our unique personality traits and experiences aka memories. Thus working on yourself can be pretty challenging, especially if you have no basic understanding and framework to start with.

Let's be honest, **therapy is expensive**, can take years of sessions, and in case you take medicines, it can be tough to find a combination that works for you, not to mention the side effects. Not everyone can afford it, and even if you can financially, it can take many years and a lot of your time to improve depending on your mental health issues and the competence of the doctor.
Like I said earlier, not every therapist will be able to help you equally, if

they cannot understand how your mind works. Resulting not only in a waste of time and resources, but potentially making irreversible choices with the skewed approach.

Although it can be important and useful, you don't always have to keep going to therapy every week or two for years, there's another approach that can be more effective in the long term. The period when you're not in therapy, which is the most prevalent in our lives, is precisely when self-development becomes a significant factor.
If we introspect and challenge our thoughts constantly, we can start working on changing ourselves. And when we have issues or feel stuck in that process, we can occasionally go to therapy to talk about those specifics and then try to implement those new solutions or methods that we came up with. It's similar to approaching your professor or boss; you seek their assistance when facing challenges with a project or topic, and once it's resolved, you return to working independently or with your colleagues.

Doing this helps you think and work independently, but also makes sure you have some form of guidance, whether it's a person or AI. Because humans, regardless of any personal issues, are pretty adept at grasping new information, they just need the right form of guidance.

We're in the era of free knowledge.

Just a few decades ago, this would have been much more difficult to achieve. You would have had to invest in multiple books with varying approaches and try them out. Besides, online resources for various topics, mental health knowledge, and other materials were often paid or not easily accessible even if they were free, making them out of reach for many people due to financial constraints.

Accessing enough funds for mental health resources and therapy can be challenging, especially for children and teenagers. And that is the most important age for mental and physical development. At 25, our brain's development reaches it's peak and eventually stagnates soon after. The knowledge and skills learned in childhood and teenage years, if done properly, will stay with the person for the rest of their lives in the form of their thoughts and habits and even make cruising through life easier, especially in terms of being adaptable to constant changes in the global world.

BUT... **your age doesn't matter**, as long as you are not fixated on your opinions and beliefs, you can change at any stage of life, your past, present, future, financial status, or personal lives don't matter. As long as you are a human, and *have a brain*, there is a way to work things out. Just like how different species of plants need different nutrients and specific environment conditions to grow in, humans, similarly, in the right environment and around the right people can keep growing throughout life. Well, there is one small difference; humans, unlike plants, are not stuck in one place. You can keep moving around jobs, cities, countries, relationships, and almost everything, until you find a place where you feel content or happy. By nature we are possibly one of the most dynamic species in our behavior and thoughts.

The only caveat would be; you'd have to give up on your family and friends if you want to keep moving around the world, in search of where you belong.

Having an open mind is not something you're born with, it's something you have to put effort in, consciously or subconsciously, and practice throughout life...

If you're among the 1.8 billion views and have watched the video of the song **Paradise** by Coldplay; it shows a little elephant among humans, feeling lost, and he would constantly escape by sleeping and dreaming about a world where he is happy and can fly. But eventually, he set on a journey with very little money, and found other little elephants faaaar away from where he lived, in the middle of nowhere, and the elephant started enjoying life again because it finally found a place where he belonged, with others like him who enjoyed doing the same things as him. And that is why a lot of humans go on vacations, take time off for mental health, among other activities like participating in their hobbies and socializing every week. We all need a change of pace when our lives become too static, because we are all born with a curse. The curse of being human, perhaps the smartest brain of any species (on earth at least), and smarter the brain, the more stimulation it needs to stay happy and productive.

Everyone is unique, and has different ways to feel stimulated. For some it could be by being workaholic, gambling, playing video games, watching movies/tv shows, listening to or playing a lot of music, shopping, reading, solving theories in quantum physics, playing sports, going to the gym, partying, and whatnot.

On the contrary:

Being alone, sleeping a lot, sleeping too less, self-harming, crying a lot, abusing alcohol or drugs, they are all activities that stimulate our brain and are mostly associated with people who have depression or other mental health issues. And for people who fail to get the stimulation that their brain needs, they end up either going further down the rabbit hole and might develop harmful coping habits, taking out their frustration of themselves or on others, or doing some wild and whacky things. But whatever the case, as evident for most people, stimulation of any kind is essential for our smart-ass brain to constantly feel that satisfaction from our lives that we all seek.

It's something I like to call **"pick your sweet poison"**, we all need to pick habits and hobbies, its just some are more unhealthy and unproductive than others, I don't see actions as black and white but rather on a spectrum i.e gray. Because actions are always the end result of your thoughts and beliefs, what we see others do is the result of a collection of thoughts and emotions throughout a person's life experience. That's why there is a saying **"seeing is believing"**, because our very smart mind can always get lost in thoughts but actions are almost always done after our mind thinks of multiple different scenarios. Our actions are either impulsive, or intentional. There is no in-between; many people who fail to overcome their anxiety usually submit to their impulsive desire and thoughts, as it seems impossible to overcome for some.

There are two kinds of people for the most part: The person who is consciously making an effort, and thinking about the consequences of his actions before doing them. The other is a person who submits to his impulsive thoughts, and thinks about the consequences of his actions later.

The latter one is more commonly found among addicts, who fail to take control of their impulsive thoughts and submit to it. I mean sure, those impulsive thoughts might give you a sudden rush of dopamine or adrenaline, but the after-effects of it are usually much worse than we think. Cheating on your partner, gambling, taking drugs, or something along those lines, all might "feel" good in that very moment as they give you a sudden rush, but usually bring nothing but adversities later on.
Many kids love doing pranks for the same reason - it adds an element of excitement and thrill to their day. It gives them a rush of dopamine, seeing someone else fall into their prepared trap, and earns them recognition among their peers. And, most of us, give up on pranking once we grow up because we realize that it's not a healthy method of getting that excitement.

Teaching kids better methods of getting the thrill they seek, benefits them a lot later in life where they will pick up healthier coping habits subconsciously as adults.

Many people do things without thinking in-depth, just because "they feel like it" but that feeling is their brain picking the poison subconsciously. For people who don't have that feeling coming automatically, they need to do a lot of introspection and work on finding that feeling again. I'd love to talk more about mental health but that might make things too long and sway me away from the focus of this book. So, lets get to the topic and see how AI chat-bots like ChatGPT and Gemini can be used to help us work on our self-development.

CHAPTER SIX

SELF-GROWTH? AI IS OUR BEST BET TO SELF-RELIANCE

Now that we learned a little bit about how our mind works in the last chapter, let's jump straight to potential actions we can take. In this chapter, I'll be talking about different approaches, and giving you the barebones for creating your own approach. Since the way we look at things keep on changing, giving you a concrete solution doesn't make sense. Once you get good at the basics of creating your approach, you'll be able to keep creating new ones with the changing times in the future. Who knows by the time you read this, there will be a lot more new additions to mental health theories.

The journey begins;

1. The first method is figuring out your personality type and then using that as a basis to create customized plans. You don't have to be a genius to figure out your thought and behavior pattern, most of us are aware of what we do and how we think to some extent. The primary aim of this test is to learn keywords associated with your behaviors and thoughts, aka personality, and then use them to create customized plans for your self-development. There is a great free website to do a little personality test that takes around 10 minutes, and I'm sure many of you might have already heard of it: https://www.16personalities.com/free-personality-test. You will then get a

short report, and you can search online for your personality type to learn in-depth about it. While this won't be 100% accurate, its a great way to get an estimate of your behaviors and thoughts, especially if you're just starting on your journey of self-development.

One thing worth mentioning, **and something I want to stress**, is: a common tendency among people is to answer questions based on their ideal perception rather than reality. As a result, often ending up with the wrong personality type.

What you think is ideal and what you actually do can be worlds apart. Irrespective of your beliefs, your response should reflect what you actually do in those situations, not what you think you should have done.

So Now that you've finished the 'test' and learned about your personality keywords from the test, you can use them in ChatGPT and Gemini to get more specific details for different aspects of your self-development plans:

Searching "Tell me about INFP" will give you a list of details about your personality traits, but don't forget you'll have to change INFP to your personality type since this is just an example.

- Now that you have an overview and a clearer idea about your personality type, it's time to move on to the next stage. That is, searching "tell me about negatives and/or drawbacks of the personality type INFP".

- With this information, you can filter out the ones that are relevant to you and eliminate the ones that you don't have. In the same way, you can search for positives in the next prompt and filter them out for your relevance. Make sure you make a list of positives and negatives that are relevant to you. You can even label each one of them from 1-10, depending on how prevalent each of the point is in your personality and life.

- If you're in a phase of career change or still figuring out your career goals, it can be useful to have a list to work out with, especially if you have no idea where to start. For this, all you have to do is search "what are good and bad careers for the personality type INFP?". While this gives a very broad range of options, it also gives your brain a clearer image of your potential life canvas, which you can then slowly start painting on. You can ask the good and bad of each job separately, to get a more detailed answer.

- You can also get recommendations for other things, such as "what are some good hobbies for INFP personality type?" or "what are some methods to be more productive for INFP personality type?". Any kind of question that you might be curious about, you can add "for INFP personality" to get answers with more chances of being accurate and that might align better with your thought process and habits. Even if your personality type and skill-set are vastly different, this connection of personality and job type help align your emotional and mental traits with *potentially* suitable jobs.

- Do keep in mind, just because your personality type says something, doesn't mean you can or cannot do it. Our personalities change throughout life, depending on our experiences, surroundings, and the people in our lives. And many of us might have skills that are completely opposite of what goes along with our personality type.
Instead of strictly following the defined rules, there are countless approaches to finding loopholes and doing things in unorthodox ways. That is, if you really wish to defy the odds and do something that you'd give up anything for.

Now that we know the basics about our personality and certain traits that apply to our personality/thought process, lets start with the second step.

2. We can use our AI chatbot friends to create plans for different parts of our lives. Such as for people who struggle with planning a daily schedule, or having plans for managing the balance of time and effort into different parts of their lives. If you want just a basic framework, and fill in the details on your own, I've uploaded a template on my website that you can download for free: njsharma.com.

- Let's say you want a very basic daily schedule for the week, you can use your preferred assistant, and type in the prompt "can you make a daily schedule for me, If I go to work at 9AM and come back home by 6PM"?. With this prompt, the chatbot will then you give a detailed planner for the entire day at different time stamps. Things such as when to wake up, when to eat, for dividing your work, and later it even adds time for your hobbies, exercise, and unwinding your mind after a stressful and busy day.

Although, this plan is very basic and vague, a lot of things in it might not be relevant to you. So, let's see how we can make a detailed planner for all the detail oriented perfectionists like me.

- For example, you're a project manager or a software developer, you can use those keywords to prompt a more specific schedule. "Can you make a schedule for me? I'm a project manager and work from 10AM to 5PM," or "Can you make a schedule for me? I'm a software developer working on developing an app."

- In the same way, you can get ChatGPT and Gemini to make you a schedule for almost all kinds of plans, and not just work. All you have to do is enter "Can you make a schedule for the day, from xx am - xx pm, and i need to do x things during the day". You can otherwise also use this format to write up your own schedule manually. To give you a better idea, here are some details that you can include:

Morning: Wake-up time, breakfast, exercise, getting ready.
Work/School: Work hours, classes, study sessions, meetings.
Lunch/Breaks: Meal time, relaxation, errands, quick tasks.
Afternoon/Evening: Work/school continued, hobbies, errands, social activities.
Wind Down: Dinner, relaxation, self-care, prep for tomorrow.

3. Another great way to improve productivity is by creating to-do lists and upgrading them constantly as we move on to different activities. It's pretty easy to make the list, in the text box just type about your activities and requirements, as well as your time-frame for the activities (it could be an estimate if you don't have the exact time). Or use this format to write it manually. For example:

- **Context:** Is this for your entire day, a specific project, or a personal goal?

- **Priorities:** Are there any urgent tasks or deadlines that need to be at the top of the list?
- **Breakdown:** Would you prefer a general list or more specific subtasks for each item?
- **Time Estimates:** Do you want to include estimated timeframes for each task?
- **Additional Notes:** Are there any specific tools or resources you need to complete the tasks.

Creating a to-do list is simple, you can also do it on your phone's notes app and sync it with cloud to access it on any device that you might own. The apps have an option for creating a to-do list and setting up reminders as well, which might work better for most people since most of us check our phones much more than our PC. Now that phones are getting smarter with better assistant and AI integration, creating reminders and lists becomes much more seamless and interactive. Notes app on Iphones and samsung are getting more and more AI integration, making it easier to create things like to-do lists.

Even if you can't check off everything on your to-do list, accomplishing some of the listed tasks every day or week is still a win, *in my book*. More often than not, people find themselves overwhelmed and unable to complete their daily and weekly tasks on time. If you're able to do even half of the tasks on your weekly/daily to-do list, you're already ahead than at least 60% of the population.

Verbal and non-verbal skills

Now that we have a better idea about our personality traits, let's move on to another essential skill that permeates every part of of our life, whether consciously or subconsciously.

Almost everyone needs these skills in order to function and thrive in society (at least to a certain minimum level, if not proficient in them). Many people tend to disregard these skills as not very crucial, because they are often improved subconsciously through regular social interaction. While these skills may not reach their full potential through solely social and informal interactions, they develop to a sufficient level to get by socially and professionally. It is one of the major reason why well-known global leaders, businessmen, celebrities, and many others have such a significant influence. Their ability to captivate others with their 'aura' is often attributed to natural talent, but in reality, they tirelessly work on enhancing their non-verbal and verbal skills throughout their entire lives, ensuring they always shine socially and publicly.

However, this is not always the case for a significant portion of the population. Today's generation and the future generations, in particular, will rely heavily on online communication, thus the development of both verbal and non-verbal skill is either stunted or delayed. This particular circumstance can be quite overwhelming as individuals, especially teenagers, are suddenly expected to use these skills without having the chance to develop a practical understanding of them in the real world. It's like throwing someone into the deep end of a pool by just showing them a video of how to swim.

For the proper development of verbal and non-verbal skills, children should have constant exposure to real-life experiences, with the guidance of adults, because verbal/non-verbal skills are perhaps one of the most complicated skills to be proficient in. The interpretation and perception of speech and behavior vary greatly among people from different cultures, personality types, economic backgrounds, races, and genders. Developing these skills requires more than just relying on books or the internet.

Similarly, adults who want to improve their skills often encounter a common challenge: they need a platform to get guidance to develop these skills. Unlike children, adults face more difficulty in finding learning opportunities at the same level of exposure. **However, there is some good news**. With the help of AI, you can kick-start your learning experience. AI can act as a personal teacher, guiding you diligently from the very beginning and continuously evaluating your progress as you gradually advance.

Non-verbal skills are considered to be over 70% of the communication process, while verbal hovering around 30%.

Regardless of your language, country, occupation, or age, non-verbal skills are the first things people see when we interact with them and having good non-verbal skills helps us in a lot more ways than we think. Imagine going up to a random person you're interested in being friends with, and your body language appears rather laid-back, it might make the person disinterested. That wouldn't be very convincing as a first impression, but at the same time if you show confidence via your body, it will potentially leave a longer lasting first impression and you might end up with a new friend.

Likewise, in a job interview, the interviewer pays close attention to your non-verbal skills, as they already have an idea of your background from your resume, making your non-verbal skills the main focus.

Another reason why some people are naturally good at making friends or getting jobs, they might have subconsciously developed their non-verbal skills to a higher level than they realize.

Achieving a balance between verbal and non-verbal skills is an important skill, and it is normal for minor imbalances to exist, as they are influenced by various factors in our daily lives. However, when these two skills become so imbalanced that they hinder your growth and progress in various areas of life, it becomes a problem. It's a lifelong process to improve and update these skills, like keeping your body in shape. There are a variety of skills under it:

1. Body language is the most widely used term when discussing non-verbal skills, and for good reason. It's about expressing your emotions and message using your body movements: facial expressions, head and shoulder tilt, gestures, physical contact like handshake and hugs, and even breathing.

- The most noticeable aspect of body language in communication is the use of facial expressions and eye contact. When you speak, people primarily focus on your face, which greatly influences their impression of you. Having some control over your facial expressions can be highly advantageous instead of relying on impulsive behavior. Particularly in the context of business communication, these skills are highly valued as they greatly impact negotiations, meetings, and your overall reputation within the organization.

- Gestures play a vital role in communicating our thoughts and messages in a more interactive manner than mere words. By incorporating movements, you can engage the audience, compelling them to pay closer attention to your words. Gestures not only help us express the meaning behind our words, but they also add depth to our emotions and reinforce the message we convey. Knowing how to use gestures is an underrated skill, both professionally and personally, for networking, socializing, presentations, selling something, and even just everyday conversations.

- The importance of posture often goes unnoticed by many people, even though it should be given more attention and not left to impulse. I think we all know what posture is, but to have good posture, you gotta put in some physical work, like exercising. Good posture serves a dual purpose - it enhances non-verbal communication, and protects you from the future back and shoulder issues that come with inevitable aging.

- Personal space is a commonly neglected aspect of non-verbal communication. But what is it exactly? Well, it is: Being mindful of personal boundaries and knowing when to initiate or avoid physical contact, such as handshakes, hugs, or shoulder taps, is the key to navigating through various social and professional situations. Moreover, the appropriate distance to maintain while talking varies based on factors like the occasion, location, gender, your immediate environment, and the people you are interacting with.

2. Vocal cues (paralinguistic) are often mistakenly grouped with verbal communication, but they are actually a component of non-verbal skills. There are several aspects to it:

- Your voice tone and volume are super important non-verbal skills. The tone plays a crucial role in delivering the message and can significantly influence how the message is perceived. Throughout history, those who have been regarded as exceptional public speakers have always possessed a profound mastery of voice modulation. It's not just about knowing when to use them, but the real challenge lies in effortlessly incorporating them into everyday life and conversations. For instance, if you ask a question in a dull and booming tone, it might come across as an irritated inquiry. On the flip side, if you ask with a softer voice and a curious tone, people will more likely take you seriously.

- The key to communication lies in expressing your message in an engaging way, rather than just speaking the words in a monotonous voice. But hey, even AI can do that, just by lifelessly saying words to get the message across. We're way smarter than those dumb AI's, so let's use it to our benefit and add some vibrancy to our speech. For instance: Singers change their voice tones to highlight different parts of lyrics. Despite using the same words, different emotions can be expressed by using varying techniques of voice modulation.

- Two other factors that influence how others perceive our speech are voice inflection and vocal variety. Inflection is the change in rise and fall of pitch in different parts. It can be used to highlight crucial aspects of your speech or signal a shift from a serious to a sarcastic tone. When a sentence is long without any emphasis, or to mark its end, the pitch falls. Moreover, at the beginning of a sentence or when asking a question to emphasize important keywords, the pitch rises. However, this can be reversed as well, so it all depends on what you're talking about and where you're at, but the general idea is to constantly change tone and make your speech more interesting to listen to.

- Speed; another part of voice inflection. Changing the speed of your speech consistently is an important factor in keeping the audience engaged and interested while maintaining their level of interest.

- Vocal variety is an umbrella term that includes things like inflection, among other things. It also covers stuff like enunciation, pauses, and a whole lot more. If you want to start an in-depth journey for speech improvements, you can further use your AI friends and then use those keywords to search for resources online; especially on YouTube and google.

- Effective pacing, strategic pauses, and minimizing fillers are key to making a lasting impression on your audience. Each speaker has their own unique style, and this remains true for well-known and influential speakers who have crafted their own distinct speech patterns. Famous public speakers such as Martin Luther King Jr, Mahatma Gandhi, Nelson Mandela, JF Kennedy, and even Adolf Hitler possessed a carefully crafted communication style designed to engage their specific target audience. Setting aside his actions, Hitler possessed exceptional oratory skills and charisma, which allowed him to gather significant support and captivate audiences wherever he went.

Not addressing the audience correctly, maintaining stiff body language, conveying unclear messages, and providing an overload of information are some of the common blunders made by inexperienced speakers. Overuse of fillers such as "um, yeah, like, you know" is another common trait.

Don't worry about taking pauses, just make sure it feels natural. If your pauses give the impression that you're unsure or have forgotten your speech, it can make listeners lose interest. But, if your pause makes you look like you are thinking really hard and about to say something very important, all eyes will be on you. Non-verbal communication is incredibly influential but can be challenging to master, particularly when addressing a diverse audience with varying perspectives, personalities, and beliefs. So, it's crucial to adapt and use different communication skills based on how the audience reacts. In business meetings or workplace, you're gonna be dealing with all kinds of people, so it's important to switch up your approach in communication to effectively present and negotiate in such a dynamic environment.

Similarly, famous individuals face the challenge of managing a vast audience, both domestically and internationally. Interacting with such a diverse range of people, with varying perspectives, cultures, beliefs, desires, and habits, is undeniably difficult. It takes a certain level of mastery to uphold your public image and continuously attract attention, and this skill must be practiced and polished throughout your entire life; otherwise, you'll be long forgotten in the depths of history.

It's in your reach!

The best part is; anyone can learn nonverbal communication skills and use them to improve their lives and minds. You might look at some people and think "wow, he really has a natural talent for communication skills". I mean, that might be true to some extent, since we all have our strengths, but that doesn't mean you can't excel at it. Being 'very good' and being 'excellent' are two completely different concepts. Developing a high level of skill is achievable for most people, regardless of natural talent, but reaching excellence often requires an inherent aptitude.

Even if you become very good at it, you'll be better off than at least 70% of the global population in communication. Nonetheless, growing our skills in communication not only facilitates our growth and enhancement, but also complements our other abilities. This is because; effective communication is a prerequisite regardless of the nature of our skills.

Consider this scenario: There are sports-persons who showcase extraordinary aptitude in their sport, surpassing a majority of their peers. However, their limited social skills and incompetence in public communication may hinder their marketability compared to individuals who might not be as good as them, but possess effective communication skills. And since professional sports is a pretty short career for most, many of them might not retain financial stability after they retire. On the flip side, someone with good communication skills might end up partnering with brands, and still earn income post-retirement.

Learning is a personal journey, and we all progress at our own speed. With tens, if not hundreds, of approaches available, there are endless possibilities to attain the desired outcome. Our only objective is to discover what aligns with our brain and a method of understanding that works for us. **Oh, and remember to not give a damn about what others say during your journey.**

Back to technology:

If you have smart-products such as watches, bands, lights, AR/VR glasses, speakers, and others, I'll be using them as part of training. These products make it so much easier to track your skills and progress. You'll know exactly how to improve and where to focus. This approach allows us to grasp and learn things from different perspectives and methods, something a human teacher might find challenging. We can learn and apply logic in our own way using technology, because who knows us better than ourselves?

I'll be giving you different examples and formats on how to use modern technology to improve your non-verbal skills. I won't simply give you techniques because they are always changing and the AI search results offer a wide range of options for individuals with different practice methods.

If I only mention specific methods, they may not be effective for everyone and could become obsolete by the time you read this. **Making the most of AI is another part of being independent.**

<u>FACIAL EXPRESSIONS</u>

Facial expressions are key to communication and you can totally practice them on your own, if you're not confident of doing it in front of others yet. But before you get started, you need to figure out how good you currently are. So, the first thing you should do is record videos of yourself. It's not only for self-evaluation, but also for keeping a record as you progress. Remembering where you started before starting your journey is crucial in acknowledging your growth and identifying any areas that may have been overlooked.

- First put your phone in-front of you on a table or an object for support, with the front-camera on to record yourself. It should be at an angle where you can not only see your entire face, but at least until your chest or stomach is ideal. You won't need it now, but I suggest making things more organized for later on. Facial expressions and body language should be in sync. So, later, when you practice body language, you can also pay attention to your facial expressions at the start of your journey and work to enhance the synergy between the two.

- Then open up ChatGPT/Gemini and type "can you give me a small paragraph to speak and practice my facial expressions?". The next step is pretty simple; just record yourself and speak how you always do. Don't try to prepare for it, because the first recording should always be how you communicate normally. (Google Gemini will give a more detailed answer)

- If you have a smartwatch, smart-band or a smart-ring, don't forget to wear it. They will help in tracking heart-rate and stress levels, and this data (if accurate) is useful to monitor different parts of recording and also to understand if you get more anxious when speaking.

- Don't forget to stand below a light, and perhaps in-front of a mirror if you want to see yourself in action. You can also dim all other lights, so the focus stays on your face. This trick can be used in all the steps, as it helps to slowly train your subconscious mind of being the focus in front of people, for when you have to present or speak in-front of an audience. **Mastering communication skills goes beyond just learning**; it involves training your subconscious mind to be aware and confident when you're around people.

- Now, you can type in ChatGPT/Gemini "give me some paragraphs to practice speaking with different expressions". This prompt will give you several different paragraphs and each associated with a different emotion to show. In front of the mirror, you can now speak each one of them and look at your face to move different parts of it for expressing emotions. For this you will need to experiment moving different parts of your face, since not everyone can move all parts fluidly. Some of the most common facial expressions are: Happiness, Sadness, Confusion, Anger, Surprised, Disgust, Fear, and Interest. You can practice each of them one by one, then slowly practice scenarios where you have to use all of them in a mix, constantly switching it up.

- Once you've practiced in front of mirror, its time to move on to the next step. You can use your favorite songs, pictures, or scenarios from movies or play. You can first watch the scenario and then imagine yourself in that situation. Then speak along as the character and give facial expressions similar to what the actor did or the song is conveying. This can be tough to do initially, but slowly you get better at it.

VOICE MODULATION

- You can type in "can you give me different techniques for practicing voice inflection?". This will give you several warm-up exercises, practice scenarios, and techniques to implement in your practice. You can then ask the prompt to expand into detail into each of these categories one by one, as you use them.

- Don't forget voice modulation and inflection are harder than they look like. Often times if we speak for a while, our voice may fluctuate or crackle because we did not warm up our vocal chords. Well, just like our body needs to warmed up before exercise, our throat needs to be too.

- For this, just type in "what are some ways to warm up your throat before a speech?". This will give you some exercises, tips and methods to warm up your vocal chords. You should try to do this everyday. Making it a regular practice will help you be ready to speak any day, especially if your work requires you to speak a lot. And don't forget, a good posture and diet is important for the optimal performance of our vocal chords.

<u>GESTURES</u>

- Gestures and posture are more co-related than you might expect. There needs to be a good balance of both for each to be effective in non-verbal communication. If you have a good posture but bad gestures, it may not convey your message properly. Conversely, if your gestures are good but posture is bad, it will not look good either. The latter is worse but an imbalance is seen as negative, especially in professional life.

- To practice gestures, you first need to know about them. for this just type in "what are the different types of gestures in communication?" additionally you can also make the question longer "what are the different types of gestures? + how can i practice them for speaking?". This will give you a list of different styles and tips to start. To learn about and practice each gesture, you can be more specific with each question.

- After that, it's all about repeated efforts and practice. One method is to practice in front of a mirror, while another is to record yourself and analyze your movements. From there, you can work on enhancing each individual movement. You can also play some music in the background and dim your lights, to set a more relaxing environment.

<u>EYE CONTACT + PERSONAL SPACE</u>

- To practice eye contact and personal space, you can start again by standing in-front of the mirror and walk towards it from a distance. Think of what a healthy distance is; not too close not too far. For formal events, personal space is considered very important while for social events you can get a pass for errors in personal distance.

- To understand more about it, just search on ChatGPT/Gemini "how to maintain a healthy personal space during communication?". This prompt will give you multiple answers for different scenarios that you can keep in the back of your mind.

- You can also ask for video explanations "can you suggest YouTube videos for personal space in communication?". While sometimes this command can give broken links, the video titles and channel names are accurate which you can use to then search on YouTube. Both our AI chat-bots save you the trouble of manually searching for popular videos, making it more convenient than trying to find decent ones on your own.

- Additionally, you can search for "What is good personal distance for professional environment?" and "What is good personal distance for social environment?". You can find a range of tips and suggestions for different environments, depending on which one you want to focus on.

- Once you've practiced these suggestions in front of a mirror, you can try them out with your friends, family, or even while shopping. These habits don't become ingrained in our minds overnight, so don't worry if you struggle with them—it's common for most people. With time, these habits will become automatic, without you needing to consciously think about them.

Picking up non-verbal skills can be a hit or miss, especially if we leave it to fate. Depending on your age, location, gender, culture, and mental health, it can be challenging for many, especially the younger generation surrounded by technology. These suggestions and tips can be very useful to go into any social environment, think of it as preparing for your interview. When you have the basics in mind, you can improvise upon them as you practice.

With that said, seeking outside help can be ever so challenging. But here's the best part, we're living in the technology era, right in the midst of an AI revolution. Once the dust settles, technology will be present in every aspect of our lives, more than we could have ever imagined. To prepare for this significant change in our lives and our pursuit of success in the outside world, we must be ready. Ready to face the sudden changes up-ahead and dealing with the uncertain things that will happen as the AI revolution grows and spreads.

To succeed in this digital era, it is crucial to make the most of technology's potential.

And what better way to learn and enhance our skills than using the very 'AI' that is threatening our jobs? If we're competing with AI, we exploit each other's strengths until one of us emerges victorious. Using AI is far beneficial than looking for ways to avoid it, and most us have a capable enough brain to adapt to these changes.

That's why there is a saying " **Where there is a will, there is a way**". Our brain has the capacity to adapt to almost everything. The only caveat is: for some people it's faster than others. You know how there are so many phone models with different features, speed, and durability. In the same way, every individual has their own set of traits and a specific tempo when it comes to achieving goals. It's a question without a clear-cut answer; the capacity of humanity resides in a gray area that flourishes when given the right conditions. Humanity's strength lies in our individuality and our ability to collaborate, using each other's strengths to accomplish the impossible.

The most common things that mess with our productivity are:

1. Emotional needs
2. Logical needs
3. Sense of security
4. Physiological needs
5. Stable income

Imagine traveling back to 2020, where the world was gripped with fear and uncertainty as the pandemic took hold and everyone scrambled to find ways to combat the unknown virus.

To mitigate the spread of the virus, countries adopted measures like travel bans, strict lockdowns, and emphasized the importance of staying indoors.

Well, what do you know? This extended period of uncertainty has had a detrimental effect on both our mental health and our ability to interact socially. Professional athletes understand the importance of consistent practice throughout their careers. Even a brief hiatus from training can result in a loss of their competitive edge. Similarly, just like our muscles, our brain requires constant training and stimulation to operate at its fullest potential. It's not only sudden withdrawal that impacts our mental health; prolonged social isolation can have a range of effects, some of which may take years to undo.

Some of the major effects that isolation can have:

- The effects of prolonged isolation extend to our sleeping patterns, diet, and decision-making capabilities. Consistent high levels of anxiety and fear can disrupt hormonal+chemical balance and also cause individuals to withdraw from things they enjoyed doing. By combining all of these elements; it creates an individual who is consistently anxious, frequently distracted, or emotionally unstable, ultimately leading to reduced productivity in their everyday life. Not only do these things affect our cognitive processes, but they diminish the quality of our verbal and non-verbal abilities. Consider this: an anxious person's discomfort becomes more evident during communication, while a confident individual who believes in themselves displays fewer signs of unease.

- Paranoia is one of the most noticeable effects of long-term isolation. One of the changes post-COVID is the pervasive fear of others and the belief that people are against us. More and more people have changed, becoming less social and choosing to spend their time indoors. This shift in behavior can be attributed, in part, to a growing sense of mistrust towards both individuals and the social environment as a whole.

- Disguised as a silent disease, loneliness poses significant threats to our overall well-being. It not only shortens our lifespan but also diminishes the quality of our emotional and physical health. Perhaps most importantly, it distorts our perception of the world, leading to the gradual deterioration of our relationships and brain's intelligence over time. Those with depression and other mental health issues have firsthand knowledge of their struggles. They witness their impulsive habits taking over, feeling trapped in a cycle that seems unchangeable. Over time, not being able to control your thoughts totally wrecks your self-confidence and self-perception. These people don't give themselves enough credit, not because they're unaware, but because their brain is playing tricks on them.

There are a lot of things that can go awry when people are isolated for long periods of time and strip off their social and personal needs. Stagnation in brain functioning and development, worsening emotional regulation, and potential deterioration of existing relationships can occur.
Among all the effects; their self-esteem, self-image, and self-confidence are the most negatively affected. These three things are invaluable and can greatly enrich a person's life. They support personal growth, foster relationships, enhance work productivity, promote professional advancement, improve cognitive function, and emotional regulation.

Use this opportunity to document your concluding thoughts on various aspects of the points I mentioned, like; your mental well-being, social interactions, and any hindrances to your professional advancement, things holding you back in different aspects of your life. Don't forget to add your best qualities to the list, too. You might wonder why I'm asking you to write positives? Trust me, it's important and will make sense, eventually. Once you have it written, you can refer back to it when needed.

<u>Updating skills</u>

These chatbots can serve as virtual therapists, offering individuals who struggle with mental health issues the opportunity to explore various answers for their worries and questions. Additionally, they can help us gain a different outlook on things, enabling us to approach situations with a more positive mindset. Although it may lack the emotional connection of therapy, this is an excellent starting point for improving your mental health, especially if you're on a tight budget.

You can ask questions such as:

- Can you give me strategies to reduce my overthinking?
- What are some ways to reduce my negative thoughts and depression?
- It can even be used for specific thoughts, just like you'd ask yourself or a therapist. "can you give me a perspective? If there are so many negative things happening in the world, why should we work hard and try for the future?". Just like this example, you can type out anything that is keeping up your smart brain occupied and ask for a different perspective.
- You can also use it to challenge your beliefs that you know are hindering your growth. Such as "can you challenge my thought: is it worth attempting new relationships if there is a high chance of rejection?". This might give you an entirely new perspective, and may give you a reason to keep trying.
- Another method to help you enhance your emotional health is by rephrasing your negative thoughts into positive ones. For example you can type; can you rephrase this thought into a positive one? "I can't do it, I'm not good enough". You'll then get many different thoughts to challenge your belief, and possibly a few different approaches to work on for changing your thought process.
- You can use it for learning about new and healthier habits. Using your personality type to get ideas about adopting new habits is worth attempting.
- You can ask these chatbots for help in dealing with mood changes.
- You can get tips to go out and make new friends, or before a big event like a presentation or a meeting.
- Almost all kinds of social and personal events and activities can be dealt with just by changing our approach. But there are tens and hundreds of methods to deal with each emotion and action. Thus, learning about all of them becomes impossible. It is more efficient to pinpoint and learn the ones that are relevant to you or for people around you. And that is where these AI chatbots come into play, in helping you to filter out and narrow down things that are more likely to work for you.

"Give a man a fish and feed him for a day, teach him how to fish and feed him for a lifetime".

I mean, you don't necessarily have to be a man, but you get the point. Relying on others, be it your partner or therapist, for every problem you face may lead to a strong dependence on them. This statement is especially applicable to individuals who are socially isolated, suffering from depression, and experiencing elevated levels of anxiety. In the eyes of the emotionally vulnerable, that particular person becomes a radiant source of light, illuminating their path through the darkness. In this way, their dependence on that person for their emotional and mental well-being could potentially increase.

Just like teaching a child to speak; once they gain confidence in their abilities and start speaking, they start trying different ways of speaking, sometimes imitating others, other times creating their own way of speaking. As we grow and become adults, we gradually become more accustomed to speaking differently in different situations and with different people. What these suggestions aim to do is provide you with a first step, offering you a direction to pursue. From there, you can immerse yourself in learning and pave your own chosen path. Expect to stumble and encounter obstacles as you progress, but with time, you will develop into a person who is self-reliant and possesses greater mastery over your own emotions.

On that note, comprehending the basics of emotions, habits, and thoughts is possibly one of the toughest things we face in life. Many people struggle to comprehend the underlying cause of their emotional reactions, leading them to engage in detrimental habits such as drinking, smoking, stress eating, self-harming, and other behaviors that can be harmful to both themselves and those around them.

Thus, this chapter. Even if my words don't personally resonate with you, they might be valuable for your friends or family who are facing challenges. We all have unique brains, experiences, and feel emotions in different ways. This is why there is never a one-size-fits-all solution, as even individuals with similar habits may have distinct logical and emotional justifications for their choices. Like the goal of avengers and thanos were similar: To make the earth a better place for everyone, but their thought-process and path completely different.

Uniqueness should be celebrated!

Embracing your uniqueness and searching for answers that help you understand things is what makes us humans, humans who have both logical and emotional capacity in a much more complex manner than any other living creature. When someone forces themselves to not express their mind because they fear judgement, they are only self-sabotaging and causing long-term damage for their future self.

The lack of physical stimulation is one of the main causes of the increasing anxiety rates among people today. And no, I don't mean just going to the gym. The internet has become the primary platform for completing tasks, whether it's through your phone or computer, and a substantial portion of our lives now occurs online.

Imagine this scenario: A kid goes to school/college at 8AM and spends the next 7 hours within the walls of classroom listening to teachers and his classmates. He comes back mentally drained due to sitting in a closed room all day, then he spends his free time on his computer, browsing the internet or playing video games. Again, within the walls of his room. After that he does his pending homework or projects. At night, the kid spends his time watching youtube or shows, then goes to sleep.

Well that's the gist of how a day looks like for a large number of kids and young adults today.

Its similar for many adults; Imagine spending your entire day within closed walls from 9-5, I mean sure you get to talk to people and socialize while also working. That's not a bad thing in itself, depending on the kind of work you do. But, once your work is over and you come home mentally tired, you just want to spend some alone time doing things online or go out with your friends for some drinks. Again, the physical stimulation that our brain and body might need may not be met. A lot of people find gym as a stress buster, but a lot of them avoid it too.

The level of physical stimulation needed varies from person to person, with some requiring higher than others. However, as humans, our bodies and minds are naturally wired for the need of physical stimulation. And it's not something we can just delete or hide. It may not be immediately apparent, but physical stimulation is essential for maintaining both our physical and mental health, promoting emotional regulation, strengthening our immune system, and enhancing our five senses.

Here's why :

- Physical exercise improves our motor stability and develops our senses as well as our eye movement. All these things require us to focus on what we are doing and in turn solidifies in our brain on how to manage our emotions, while also focusing on the task we're doing that requires our attention.

- It improves our cognitive abilities, making on the spot decisions, relying on different senses as well as improving our reaction time to things that are happening right in-front of us.

- Regular exercise has a significant impact on improving our sleep patterns, although the degree of improvement may vary among individuals. For example: Many sports like football, baseball, cricket, tennis, squash etc. Not only do you have to stay completely focused on the ball, but you also have to make instant decisions in the heat of the moment. These things help our brain develop the ability to make decisions even when stressed or exhausted.

- Various research studies conducted across different countries consistently link poor physical and mental stimulation to cognitive decline in aging individuals. You can request your preferred chat assistant for sources on these extensively studied and reviewed research papers/studies by experts and doctors worldwide. Or just talk to a doctor, the old-fashioned way.

- Running for 30 minutes a day can reduce moderate depression by up-to 20%. The best part is, it's free and won't give you any side effects like medications. A regular and consistent exercise routine has shown long-term effectiveness in reducing anxiety and depression, improving cognitive ability, and lowering the risk of dementia and poor memory.

- Engaging in physical activities demands full concentration from both your mind and body, and as we begin, our attention gradually becomes more focused on the activity. When it comes to playing sports, the warm-up phase serves a crucial purpose. It is not limited to merely heating up our bodies, but also involves a gradual mental transition, allowing our minds to fully engage in these activities while disregarding any other distractions. This is why people sometimes spend over an hour warming up before getting into the game. Lack of concentration on sports or alternative exercise can lead to an increased risk of injuries and subpar performance compared to our usual standards.

- Regular physical activity contributes to a greater release of endorphins, which in turn assists in soothing our brain and muscles. It is not a permanent fix, but there never will be. Similar to anti-depressants and anxiety medications, which require regular, long-term usage.

So yes, I think this chapter made a lot of things clear for you. For the things it didn't; you can ask chatbots for immediate answers.

Consistently exercising, whether at the gym or playing sports, can help reduce the stress caused by work, relationships, or other aspects of life. It may not work the same for everyone. For example: some sports fail to make me interested, while others make me so immersed that i forget everything else. Gym especially is boring for me, because I like speed and need something to focus on at all times; like a ball.

Especially in kids and young teenagers, sports/martial arts is essential because their brains and body are still developing, and full of energy.

Just like how we have different apps for different moods and various music and movie/tv show preferences depending on how we feel at the moment, it is important to have multiple hobbies and relationships in our lives to have something to immerse ourselves in. When those instinct based emotional needs are neglected and left unexpressed, they can manifest in destructive ways such as depression, anxiety, unhealthy eating patterns, substance abuse, and reliance on other dependencies.

CHAPTER SEVEN

MAKE AI A FRIEND, BEFORE IT BECOMES A FOE!

In this chapter I'll be talking about the different ways that technology can be implemented in our lives, not just by ourselves, but others such as: Institutions, Governments, businesses etc. For true self-development, we need to be aware of the world we live in, "self"-awareness alone isn't enough to thrive in our complex society. I'll also be giving different perspectives and some potential suggestions to deal with these changes.

Since you've made it till here, let me share a secret with you. AI also possesses the power to influence and manipulate people, depending on how it's used. However, that term carries many negative connotations. So instead, we'll be using it for 'persuasion'.

Emphasizing: Self-development is not just working on yourself.

No matter how much we work on ourselves, we cannot disregard our humanity. Meaning; we all feel fear, loneliness, anger, confusion, thrill, and all those emotions. No matter if you're the smartest person in this world, or the most patient, you cannot escape the complex emotions that humans are born with.

For instance: Many singers sing about their struggles or anger, and for them, it is an outlet for releasing all their stress. While doing so, they combine it with music and sell it. This method of outlet can be considered far healthier than many others. But, we should always have multiple outlets, and not just depend on one. Because, when we don't have access to that one outlet, **then we risk emotions taking control of our mind.**

And so, working on yourself is merely half of the process, the other half comprises many factors such as the shift in social & global trends, industries, and technology; to sum it up: it includes everything happening around us in the world. Something that we saw happen at a global scale and rather aggressively from 2019 to 2023.

Regardless of how much personal growth and development you may have achieved in the preceding years, nobody could have anticipated the magnitude of the pandemic and the subsequent impact it would have on key industries, technology, and consequently, global economies and job markets. Global wars and worsening job markets added to the growing anxiety, while the rising costs of basic necessities and tech products only intensified the feeling of financial strain.

The weight of the responsibility to secure and maintain employment, while also providing for the lifestyle you and your family are accustomed to, is a constant pressure. Additionally, there was the added pressure of saving sufficient funds to cover medical emergencies during a worldwide health crisis. The cumulative mental strain from various factors intensifies over time, and with the implementation of lockdowns, the instability further escalates, exacerbating the stress experienced by many.

Self-awareness and emotional intelligence are valuable assets during tough times, also known as mental fortitude.

Imagine this scenario:

We are all trapped in the middle of a vast ocean, surrounded by boundless water in every direction. Our only option is to keep moving forward, navigating an unknown route, in the pursuit of reaching a resource rich land.

Some people will be equipped with better ships and advanced equipment to reach their goals, while others may have to make do with smaller boats or cheap equipment. We all come into this world with our own unique privileges, that's just how it is. However, we're all stuck in the same endless ocean. What we can do, though, is collaborate and harness each other's unique qualities to make progress and ultimately reach our destination.

When faced with the powerful forces of the ocean and its winds, we are all rendered helpless. Although we lack control over the ocean, we can still educate ourselves about its behavior. Once we have accomplished that, we can confidently guide our ships towards our destination, minimizing the chances of drowning and ensuring a successful arrival towards land.

The same concept can be extended to our lives; acknowledging that we cannot always dictate our environment or circumstances, but we can enhance our understanding to make more strategic decisions for a better future. One useful skill for that is manipulation, err, I mean persuasion, especially if your work relies majorly on conversing with people. Persuasion is one of the key skills mastered by many influential figures in business and politics. Of course, not everyone can be convinced, and you will encounter many individuals who disagree with you. However, persuading the right people can greatly contribute to your personal growth in various aspects of life.

Since technology has come so far, why not leverage it?

In the past, persuasion heavily depended on your spontaneous and interpersonal abilities, and to a large extent, it still does. However, with the widespread presence of AI and technology, it has become somewhat easier to use these skills, even if you are not highly proficient in them. A lot of skills and knowledge that seemed inaccessible in the past are now at the tip of our fingers, just a few clicks away.

Here are some instances where persuasion is really useful:

1. Negotiations.
2. Advertising & sales.
3. Business meetings and conversations.
4. Selling ideas as an entrepreneur, especially in raising funds and convincing talent to join your company.
5. Interpersonal relationships and resolving conflicts.

6. Politics & social movements.
7. Job interviews, networking with all kinds of people, no matter the place.

Being able to communicate effectively with others, whether at home or elsewhere, is important in many ways. Developing persuasive skills is also essential for ensuring that you are not taken advantage of or manipulated by others who may try to dominate conversations or try to make you agree to what they want.

How can we improve our persuasion skills? Well, it's the old fashioned way...

1. Learn
2. Practice
3. Note down our mistakes and shortcomings(introspect)
4. Improve our mistakes
5. Practice
6. Repeat

Especially in the beginning stages, when mistakes are frequent.

To learn about persuasion, however, there can be a variety of tools:

1. Online courses for persuasion or influence are a great place to start, there are both free and paid courses online. Many business related courses for leadership and influence include persuasion, since that is an essential skill for anyone who wants to lead or manage people.
2. Podcasts, books, and audiobooks are another great source of learning and listening to different perspectives on how influencing works. You can find a variety of podcasts focused on business communication and leadership, which is a great place to start. Although do remember to first to a proper review check on podcasts, since there has been an influx of low quality content.
3. YouTube offers a wealth of debates and negotiation videos that serve as a great starting point for anyone wanting to improve their persuasion skills. Especially watching influential politicians and business

individuals, it is fascinating to observe their unique communication styles. By observing their body language, noticing changes in their speech and tone throughout the video, one can gain valuable insights into the mechanics of effective communication. Whether you agree with their stance is a different story, but the reason for their popularity is always because of their ability to woo a large portion of the population.

4. Use social media to look at the popular posts and comments in different categories and genres like: business, technology, science, politics etc. There are a variety of posts and discussions on them. Almost all major social media handles post regularly with the latest news in their respective category. The only downside of social media is that you'll have to filter through all the trolls, sarcastic, and ragebait comments. Since many social media websites pay for the views you bring in, people post negative opinions on purpose, to create a controversy and make money off it. Something people like to call 'ragebait'.

You can then practice your newly learned knowledge in your life. For example talking on the phone, or when you're out shopping for groceries, even talking with your friends or family. Any scenario that involves some form of communication, you can use any of the techniques that you might have observed or learned online.

Beyond influencing others; Persuasion shapes self-image and motivates action.

I'm sure you must have heard of the term "fake it till you make it". Well, the premises of that phrase is based on constantly persuading yourself that you can make it big. Keep persuading yourself until you finally reach your goal. In theory, that helps with self confidence, but it can have side-effects to it.

It is a double edged sword. People are more prone to over-estimating their skills and knowledge if they try to 'fake it' too much, so proceeding with caution while also faking it is a far better approach. Faking it can be particularly beneficial for individuals struggling with low self-esteem and confidence.
BUT,
If you develop a habit of faking it, you could also end up as one of those

egoistic people who constantly boast about themselves and believe they are superior to others, thus reducing your growth rate and potential. Unless you walk the talk, many people could lose trust in your abilities as time goes on.

Let's talk about some important topics that are rather essential for a satisfactory life:

<u>Emotional intelligence</u>

Venturing away from persuasion, there's another skill that is considered really useful, and that is... emotional intelligence. By practicing it, you can effectively control your own emotions and gain the ability to perceive the emotions of those around you. The second part is very important, especially in business communication.

Understanding emotions of others during a meeting or negotiation, on-the-spot, is crucial in getting that sweet deal you were hoping for.

As I mentioned in the last chapter, using your emotional skills along with persuasive techniques can propel you forward in your career, personal relationships, and even in regulating your own emotions. Building healthier relationships, managing conflicts more constructively, and experiencing the positive impact of your efforts, all contribute to a significant reduction in day-to-day mental stress. Being able to communicate your message effectively, overtime, helps you in improving your self-confidence and thus, enabling you to progress further in whatever it is that you're doing in your life.

For persuasion to work, it has to be a two-way street. When the other person feels heard, understood, and noticed, is when they become emotionally invested in the conversation and pay more attention to your words. The same applies to relationships; it's just how emotions function for the majority of people. In a conversation, everyone wants to feel important and heard. If someone feels like they couldn't speak their mind at an important event like an interview, conference, or a meeting, they might end up feeling unsatisfied or bummed afterwards.

Imagine you wanted to speak something but were not able to at that moment, or didn't get the chance to; most of us would feel a little sad about it afterwards.

AI and hardware have paved the way for a new era of communication, where real-time interaction combines multiple technologies. Imagine you're wearing smart-glasses (that look like normal glasses), with information exclusively visible to you. During your speech or presentation, you have the advantage of seeing bullet points, data visualization, and other visual elements directly in front of you as you speak and have more control over the audience. This seamless experience allows you to leverage technology to compensate for any previously lacking skills in your presentation or communication.

Therefore, individuals who become proficient in modern technology and incorporate it into different aspects of their lives will not only gain a competitive edge but also acquire skills that would be otherwise inaccessible.

An illustrative example would be: people who have a tendency to forget speech structure while speaking at important events. In such cases, smartwatches can be really useful for setting up a countdown with reminders at constant intervals. By doing so, individuals can stay on track and remain cognizant of when their speech is reaching its conclusion, enabling them to wrap up their thoughts effectively and avoid any abrupt endings.

It's a straightforward process: time your speech during practice, set reminders for each interval where you need to shift topics, and set corresponding reminders on your phone. Just moments before your crucial presentation, start the countdown on your smartwatch. And Voila, at each interval, your smartwatch will vibrate, providing reminders to help you stay on track and maintain the smooth flow of your prepared speech.

The problem with technology's excessive presence in our lives….

Many of the challenges faced by today's 'tech generation' revolve around humanistic skills such as: social, communication, and emotional skills. These skills require either 50% knowledge and 50% practice, 70% social exposure and 30% knowledge, OR 70% knowledge and 30% exposure. While these approaches may vary greatly, they ultimately lead to similar results varying on your routine, lifestyle, and dedication. Disregarding either of knowledge or real life exposure, would just reduce your growth. Some of them are slower, while others are faster.

The practice part however is the most important. If we implement it:

A. In the wrong place
B. Around the wrong people
C. At the wrong time

Then these skills might fail to bear fruit, and we might think that our efforts were in vain. The place, situation, and the time of speech are all co-related and saying things that don't fit in all 3 would confuse a lot of people rather than impress them.

Nevertheless, even with excellent knowledge and skills, there may be times when you struggle with them. What sets influential people apart is their ability to effectively employ their skills when the odds are against them, boldly defying doubts and solidifying their authority in humanistic skills.
This is why many scammers manage to deceive even well-experienced people who are accustomed to dealing with scams. Your social and human skills can take you far in many areas of life. They're like the perfect compliment to all your other skills and hobbies. Some of the most famous and controversial humans throughout history have had an ability to convince people on a large scale.

It is not uncommon for your colleagues to possess comparable skill-sets or potential, but the ability to showcase your talents in the ideal environment and at the opportune moment, greatly contributes to your career progression. Humans (well, most of them), being social creatures, are easily captivated by individuals who exhibit exceptional social skills. And it's something we can educate ourselves on, but most of us are hard-wired to be lured towards people who show exceptional communication skills. I'm not saying you need to be a master at these skills, but even having a moderate-level of proficiency in them sets you apart from the majority of global population, giving you a competitive edge in various aspects of life and work. Most famous leaders throughout history have had a certain charisma and assertiveness, that attracted the masses.

<u>Self-image and self-esteem</u>

These two are the main components of your self-confidence. Meaning, if you're just starting out your journey of improving and learning about mental health, these two are the first things you should work on. Mess up the basics and you'll end up with problems in the long-run that could turn into bad habits and thoughts.
With that in mind, lets begin!

How we see ourselves and how others see us shapes our self-confidence. It's a combination of both, even though many people may try to convince you that the latter part is worthless, but that is absolutely untrue. In reality, things don't always go as planned because we're constantly influenced by others and our surroundings. Even animals act differently around different people.

How you deal with such diverse people is the difference that sets people with high self-worth apart.

As an example: picture yourself going to school every day and experiencing the frustration of your teachers consistently blaming you for your mistakes instead of providing the necessary guidance and support to help you solve them. Over the years of constantly being blamed and criticized, your self-confidence inevitably suffers. On the contrary, envision a scenario where a child attends a school in which teachers not only assist them in problem-solving but also provide support and encouragement whenever they make errors, thus motivating the students to continuously challenge themselves and enhance their abilities. That kid will, in all probability, have a stronger sense of confidence when it comes to showcasing their abilities and emotions, resulting in greater emotional and mental fulfillment. And not just confidence, people who've had a negative experience in childhood, even if they become successful, are more prone to developing unhealthy coping mechanism as they grow older.

And this isn't just limited to kids. As an adult, living in proximity with toxic family members, friends, or in a toxic workplace can have detrimental effects on your potential for growth and progress. Not only does it drain you emotionally and mentally, but it also directly impairs your productivity, mental health, physical health, and the overall quality of your relationships with others

The famous saying **"surround yourself with positive people"** was born from a similar perspective. When we intentionally choose to be around people who possess qualities like a positive mindset, high emotional intelligence, good listeners, have high empathy, and effective time management, we open ourselves up to growth and improvement in all areas of life. Whether it's a professional, social, or personal skill, as long as we have the privilege of being in the company of someone who surpasses us in something, we will inevitably pick-up their habits and learn from them, whether it's a conscious or subconscious effort.

True self-confidence is derived from accomplishments, not solely from one's thoughts. However, what positive thinking helps with is leaving behind any setbacks and focusing on the next opportunity to try again. When people fail, they often feel stuck and lose the motivation to try again. But those who stay positive are more likely to accept failure and keep trying.

Again, it's a mix of things and not just one or the other. The emphasis on this point is for people who might question if positive thinking is worth the effort. Given that positive thinking does not come naturally to the majority of people, we must consciously strive for it and invest our emotions and energy in the ongoing pursuit of positivity. After a series of failures, one might begin to doubt the value of their efforts.

Well, failures are ALWAYS worth it.

Each failure provides an opportunity to identify the patterns, behaviors, and skills that contributed to your lack of success. Once you've taken the time to reflect and improve your knowledge and skills, you're better equipped to deal with stress and changes. You can now approach things again, going in hot with a revised strategy.

Many people, including well-known figures, have resorted to harmful coping mechanisms like smoking, drinking, and drug use. One major reason this happens is because, when people drown in success for too long, set unrealistic standards, and suddenly experience a few failures, they find it hard to accept and thus look for habits to cope with the mental stress of not being able to achieve their unrealistic standards.

Given that humans, all of us, are restricted by the biological, physical, and mental boundaries associated with our bodies, it is not reasonable to expect any individual to take on every task. The key is to have friends/colleagues who can snap you back to reality and are good at things you're not. By doing that, you can complement each other's skills and make progress towards a common goal.

CURIOSITY

It's interesting how conversations about mental health rarely touch upon the importance of curiosity. The drive to constantly search for new solutions, whether for personal growth or to aid others, is fueled by curiosity. Similar to how a doctor diagnoses illnesses, your curiosity can help you diagnose your own life, enabling personal growth and progress towards your goals.

When we are children, we tend to ask a lot of questions, engage in silly behavior, and eagerly experiment with anything that captures our interest. **But...**
Curiosity is not confined to childhood; it continues to be beneficial and relevant throughout adulthood and beyond. Given that technology and the outside world are constantly changing, it is crucial that our personality and thoughts also continue to evolve. Without curiosity, we risk being left behind in the face of this rapidly changing world.

So, heres how you can use technology to provoke your thinking:

- Combining technology and physical interactions. For instance, you can consider smartwatches, smartphones, and even the newly developed AR glasses with AI capabilities. With AR, people can receive helpful tips and suggestions in real time, enriching their interactions with others. Just picture yourself in a crucial meeting, where your smart-glasses provide you with instant tips to enhance your speech or body language, or even remind you of crucial points that you might have overlooked otherwise.

What sets these suggestions apart is that they allow you to carry on with your tasks seamlessly, without any need to pause or divert your attention, in contrast to smartphones or watches that require your full focus on their screens. Although it will be some time before it becomes practical, we can already observe the emergence of AR with products like Apple Vision Pro and some other smart-glasses that are still impractical for an average person.

- Tracking your habits and schedule is just one more thing that modern technology has made possible. You can download a planner app on your phone, or get a physical printout. I'll have a basic planner on my website as well.

- Once you have that, you can carry the daily tracker with you, and fill it out periodically. If not, you can also record data on your phone, and fill it in when you have the time. Once you have recorded data for a period of at least three weeks, you can begin identifying any irregularities in your habits and pinpointing areas that can be optimized or altered to boost productivity.

- I know following a schedule is hard, and that is why it's more practical to record your everyday schedule as it happens, then you can look for irregularities and improve upon whatever suits your preferences. These minor adjustments over-time, are very effective, but take much longer than just following a fixed schedule.

- Positive reassurance is another useful practice, that can be leveraged thanks to the power of internet. In times of stress, you have instant access to reassurance and affirmations through your smartphone. You can open my website on your phone, and save the "quotes" webpage on your home screen. You can then sort out quotes by your issue; if you're anxious, depressed, stressed, feel alone, feel sad/angry, or feel lost. I'll keep adding and shuffling regular updates to it, as time progresses. At the tip of your fingers, open up the quotes anytime you're looking for something to provoke your thoughts and get you going again.

- When you make it a habit to reassure yourself every time you feel stuck, those positive affirmations gradually become embedded in your mind. After a certain period of time, whenever you encounter similar obstacles, these affirmations automatically spring to mind, becoming natural habits.

From sports to social activities, work to education, family to acquaintances, and nearly every aspect imaginable, technology offers countless opportunities for integration and enhancement. These are just a few examples of the many, in which technology can be used. Integrating AI into our daily routines and leveraging its capabilities can give us an advantage in our pursuit to **Get ahead**.

<u>World Awareness!</u>

The secret step in self-development that no one talks about: World-Awareness. As long as we live in this world, our growth is not solely determined by our actions, but also by the circumstances that are out of our control. The extent to which an individual can achieve their goals and aspirations is heavily influenced by their ability to understand the perspectives, actions, and behaviors of others, as well as their awareness of major happenings around their country, localities, and the world.

Imagine reading news about significant shifts in the global economic policies, analyzing the potential outcomes, and investing in gold with the expectation of its value soaring. Voila! Your anticipation was correct - the value of gold is on the rise. If you made a conscious effort to stay uninformed about global politics, you would have missed the opportunity, more than likely.

That is what we call a '**calculated risk**,' a decision made not only with your intellect but also by staying informed about external events and the outside world, then combining the two. You can never be 100% sure about anything, so we all take calculated risks and keep moving forward in life. The scenario with gold is rather vague, just to give you a rough indication of how learning about the various things happening around us can help in making informed decisions for the future.

Different people have different priorities when it comes to expanding their knowledge and skills. Let's say, for a student, it might involve guessing the important topics for upcoming exams, while for an adult, it could mean delving deeper into the latest trends in their respective industry to make sure they don't get left behind in their career. Likewise, for a business owner, staying informed about the latest global consumer & market trends is important to compete, and so on.

In the same way,

Self-development goes beyond just focusing on ourselves; It might seem as though something is lacking on your part, but it could just be a compatibility issue with the ongoing trends.

Not every place will appreciate our skills, knowledge, and presence. Feeling out of place significantly impacts a person's self-perception. Imagine this teenager who's an absolute beast in athletics, but he's living in a town where people think pursuing sports/athletics as a career is a joke. Without help to develop his potential, he might end up losing his self-confidence and have lifelong self-image issues. However, if he ventures out to explore, he might stumble upon a place where sports is celebrated and treated as a legitimate profession, giving him the opportunity to monetize his talents. He feels a sense of satisfaction and acceptance, finally able to utilize his full potential and leave a lasting impression among people, in a place that truly values and recognizes his abilities.

When your abilities go unrecognized in any line of work, it can have a detrimental impact on how you perceive yourself.

A complete approach to self-improvement and self-development should open up opportunities for constant personal growth and progress in the future, rather than short-term solutions that only focus on oneself.
It is biologically impossible to learn everything on your own. That's the rationale behind companies recruiting for multiple positions and establishing different departments. In the same way, surrounding ourselves with smart and positive people helps us greatly in learning about the world around us and to keep up with the latest knowledge and trends.

I'm not a know-it-all, but I can give you some pointers on how technology will be present in different aspects of life. Being aware of these practices, that might already be in place, is essential in **Getting ahead**. So let's begin with the most prevalent topic in our lives, and globally.

Politics:

Now, I'm not gonna get into details of left or right, or pick a side for that matter. I'm going to talk about how technology can be used by politicians to influence us, as random citizens. **So let's begin:**

Politicians around the world are recognizing the immense power of AI, not only for its content creation and replication capabilities, but also for its ability to provide predictions, statistics, and algorithms that can sway people's choices, solidifying its position as the most influential tool available(yet).
The global impact will be clear, as governments around the world will utilize AI in diverse ways. Again, AI is an umbrella term for a vast amount of devices that will use different applications of it.

- Facial recognition, which is widely regarded as one of the most significant applications of modern AI, has gained notoriety as a controversial technology. By implementing AI-enabled cameras nationwide, governments can effectively monitor and identify every person whose face is captured by these advanced surveillance systems. This technology allows for real-time monitoring and instant tracking of every citizen's behavior and information. In addition, depending on the level of corruption in the country, the police can potentially run your facial recognition data through their devices to access all of your personal information, which can have either positive or negative implications.
  Imagine a futuristic scene straight out of a movie, where drones equipped with cameras swarm the skies, actively monitoring and recognizing individuals in public as they go about with their day. If a person flagged on a watch-list or wanted list is spotted, the drones swiftly relay their location to the police or government. If we're talking about catching a criminal, this tech is really handy. But, if a corrupt government gets their hands on it, they can use it to silence their critics and enforce restrictive laws, while also blocking attempts of democratic protests against those laws. In essence, it would make people believe that everyone is on board with these laws and supports the government

because everything looks so peaceful and orderly.

- AI has proven to be invaluable in the task of analyzing the extensive data being accumulated, allowing for faster and more effective categorization and summarization than ever before. Picture a hypothetical situation in which the data of an entire nation's population is extensively examined, and subsequently organized into separate categories based on their income, religion, social habits, family history, etc. This strategy can, in turn, enable politicians to strategically tailor their next election campaign towards specific demographics and manipulate people.

  However, you have to disguise these practices behind some useful features. So, imagine if the government wants to gather facial data from citizens throughout the country. They could put facial recognition on public transport, so you can just use your face to pay for tickets, by looking at scanner, seamlessly while getting in&out of the vehicle. With this particular feature, the government can effortlessly gather and retain data from millions of people, without facing any scrutiny, and subsequently, they can utilize this newly collected data in conjunction with existing government records, for purposes that go beyond just processing ticket payments.

- Low-orbit satellites are increasingly being adopted/developed to provide network connections for IoT devices and phones throughout the country. This is particularly beneficial because it eliminates the need for wire layouts, especially in difficult terrains. On the other hand, these satellites have the capability to secretly fuel surveillance devices, remaining completely inconspicuous. By leveraging internet satellites, surveillance devices have the ability to clandestinely gather and transmit data from multiple locations across a country, allowing for covert monitoring of citizens. Much like how you see in sci-fi movies, where your every movement is being tracked by random flying devices.

- Modern AI algorithms excel at selectively presenting people with specific types of content. The uses of this technology include censoring content, tracking users and putting them on a watch-list based on their post history by targeting certain keywords as red-flags, and allowing politicians to leverage this data for their election campaigns and to influence public opinion, among other possibilities.

With the use of modern AI devices, targeted election campaigns, policy formation, and categorization of citizen data based on income, religion, gender, and other resources will be more precise and widespread.

However, these features can be used in many good ways as well. Some examples are controlling crime rates, obtaining precise demographic data for more effective policy-making, enhancing infrastructure and future-proofing it, promoting equitable resource distribution, and improving disaster management response time.

In the right hands, AI can become a method of governance that is far more effective, accurate, and faster in its execution than humans. In the wrong hands, it can be used to influence people, control them, and constantly monitor their behavior.

The way it's used will vary depending on the person implementing the technology, and collectively, people hold the ability to shape these changes to a significant degree, if not entirely.

<u>Deepfakes</u>

Alongside other advancements, generative AI has introduced the world to deepfakes, a remarkable and controversial application of modern AI. Deepfakes are computer generated images or videos of people that not only look realistic but also mimic their mannerisms, voices, and expressions.

The dangerous potential of deepfakes lies in their ability to be employed by scammers, politicians, and companies as a means to propagate fake news and manipulate public perception through deceptive advertisements. Deepfakes are incredibly realistic, making it difficult for most people to distinguish between what is real and what is fake. As time passes, it'll get more realistic and harder to tell apart.

- We've already seen deepfakes of celebrities and politicians being used, for creating explicit images and videos, that become viral on social media.

- Voice replication is another feature of generative AI. Along with a fake video, you could create realistic sounding voice of that person. Example: If someone replicates a famous politician in a video, then replicates his voice to tell people to visit a malicious website, or tell them to do whatever. On the contrary, someone could deepfake your voice, call your family and talk to them in your voice asking for money.

- Deepfakes are capable of reproducing a person's fingerprint, even with just a normal image of someone, as long as their hand is visible in the picture. This gives rise to another concern, since people's pictures can be easily obtained from their social media accounts. Although it will take some time for this application of deepfake to become widespread, inevitably, it will eventually reach a larger audience. However, it's not only fingerprints that can be replicated; even our iris can be recreated using available images. All biometrics are hackable with enough resources, data, and compute power available.

- Due to the international level threat posed by deepfakes, countries are actively collaborating to develop methods for identifying and combating them. Something that many people like to call today as "fake news".

Military

The military gear these days is all about technology, and AI is gonna be in more and more of it as we move forward. Slowly, AI is going to creep into every possible equipment directly or indirectly.Your helmets? AI powered, your guns? AI powered, your planes and helicopters? AI powered, your vests and boots? AI powered.

And it's going to happen pretty soon. OpenAI, Microsoft, Google, IBM, Amazon, all have contracts with the US government to make AI enabled equipments, cloud solutions, consultancy for IT, and weapons for the military. These companies hold immense technology patents, resources, and talent, to convert these ambitions into a reality, ahead of every other major military.

Overall, a lot of technologies from the military trickle down into other industries.

The advancements and development of Jet engines, Radar, Electronic computers, rapid advancements in sonar for detecting enemies, and penicillin to name only some of the countless innovations that happened during the two world wars.

Now, calm down, I'm not even remotely hoping for a world war, but, advancements in military equipments have a lot of benefits for other industries. Take, for instance, the development and manufacturing processes employed in military equipment. These methods can be leveraged to produce safer vehicles for the general public or to create better, more efficient chips that eventually make their way into consumer tech products.

We'll have to wait and see how different countries use these fancy technologies, but we can still keep an eye on what's going on and get ready for what's coming. **In today's digital age, nothing stays private for too long.**

Education

This is something I am highly optimistic about. I believe AI, on a large scale, will "Make education fun again". The combination of modern hardware and software has the ability to revolutionize education, making it more interesting and interactive than ever before. Gone are the days of just looking at diagrams, printed text, and even staring at the computer screen to learn things.

- AI can be tailored and customized to suit the individual learning style of each student. Because every individual has a unique learning style; ensuring that every child comprehends a concept in the same manner is impossible. Children who don't understand in school either end up looking for after-school lessons, or self-teach using online resources. Thus, AI will help customize teaching and explanation methods for each student and learn their pattern to adapt individually.

- Technologies like AR, VR, and Hologram will make learning a lot more immersive. Although it will take several years for these technologies to become mainstream and cheaper. Especially for students who have a hard time visualizing things.

- Imagine you're in a class, and the teacher is talking about chemistry, which you're not necessarily fond of, because all the words just go over your head. But now imagine this: the entire structure of chemicals, along with all the information that the teacher is blabbing about, is visualized right in front of you, in the form of a hologram. It shows every important topic in detail, labelled and with more precision than just the words. Now you have this image filled in your mind, about how the things work, thus creating more incentive for your brain to recall this topic in the future when you might need to remember it, in exams or in a conversation. But, this is just one of the endless examples possible.

- Real time feedback via custom trained AI models, curated separately for each subject is another useful feature. Its impossible for teachers to physically reply to each student throughout the day, since everyone studies at different times and at their home. Thus, having some kind of instant communication for queries about a problem, in a subject, becomes necessary, especially to make sure the child stays immersed in his studies rather than giving up on it due to not finding answers. These AI software should ideally be trained by schools, according to their content and courses, making the question/answers more accurate than generic AI chatbots.

- AI powered devices can be very useful for special needs children, and adults alike. With personalized learning, and devices fine-tuned to cater to specific needs of different disabilities, AI can adapt much faster and accurately as a tool of assistance. It can also help to make people with disabilities more independent, in the sense that they will be able to do more things on their own with the help of AI devices, and rely on others for fewer tasks. Which can be a great confidence booster and make them feel empowered, *depending on their personality of course.*

- Another application could be for the teacher to track each student's progress, and identify areas where the student is struggling. This helps the teacher to improvise and adapt their teaching methods to make sure students are able to improve their weaknesses and don't fall behind. This also reduces the human effort required to monitor every student individually.

Once again, you'd have to manually customize these devices and software for each class, depending on the student data. Otherwise, there is a high chance that AI will exhibit bias, potentially leading to a decline in student performance and development.

Another risk of relying too heavily on technology is that it can become the primary method of learning, when it should only be used as a supplementary tool. Childhood plays a vital role in shaping an individual's lifelong learning journey, as it lays the foundation for future growth and development. Therefore, it is crucial to ensure that children do not develop a dependency on technology; instead, they should utilize it effectively to enhance their abilities, increase productivity, and foster self-reliance by improving their own skills.

<u>**Social media detox**</u> (And perhaps internet detox, If you dare do the impossible!)

I mean, technically you can't really live without internet in the modern world. But social media detox is still very possible. Using internet as a tool to be productive or learning, is never bad, no matter how much you rely on it. But, social media is an entirely different dimension of internet.
At times, if you accidentally end up in the wrong streets, it can become a ceasepool of toxicity and misinformation. That is why, it is always healthy to take constant breaks from social media. Just like somedays you just relax at home, after a very stressful week.

Social media detox has a lot of benefits:

- It slowly trains your mind to think for itself, rather than constantly looking at what other people think, before forming your own opinion based on what others say.

- I know I mentioned earlier, about how social media is useful to see what other people think, but listening too much to outside noise is harmful, in the same way listening too less is. Thus, to maintain your mind's sanity, constant breaks from social media are useful. Just like most jobs give you at least one day off to relax.

- Change of perspective is another thing that happens when you do a social media detox. Frequently switching up our static life is important to make sure our mind doesn't become one tracked. When we get off social media, and instead do something else like going outside, talking more with people, or even just watch sports/movies/documentaries, literally anything else that we usually don't as much, then our mind will gain a fresh perspective on various things.

- Doing tasks, that we've been avoiding and putting off for later can be done during this period of detox. You can use internet to do new courses, watch educational videos, or even clean your room!

Besides, it's a good idea to take regular breaks from scrolling through social media. Social media algorithms are intentionally designed to manipulate emotions, driving users to consume more content and make emotionally-driven choices when sharing their opinions. The better it becomes at predicting your patterns of engagement, the more extreme content it will display, with the intention of provoking an emotional response and encouraging arguments with others. As a result, social media companies experience an increase in both traffic and data, which is then reflected in their earnings reports.

The one thing we should always remember, when we are on social media, is that we are the product. In the eyes of companies, we are nothing more than a tiny speck, a statistic that investors and board members examine on their excel sheets. Spending time and energy on random internet users is often pointless, as many of them hide behind anonymity to purposefully waste your time and engage in annoying behavior to provoke you. Whenever we feel angry or sad while using social media, we should keep in mind that the platform purposely displays such content to encourage our continued participation.

However, once we understand these things, and understand the basics of how the algorithm works, we can use it to our advantage, and in turn use social media to grow our own content and influence.

Not only in real life, but in social media as well, most of us are divided into two main categories: Either be played by others, or become a player. Just to give you an idea: Influencers act as the main players, taking advantage of social media algorithms, while their massive number of followers merely consume and share the content, unknowingly being manipulated by both the influencers and the platform.

Online Security

With the rise in AI and connected technologies, data security is one of the biggest threat.
The value of user data has skyrocketed in the past 5 years, and is expected to continue its upward trajectory in the future. Companies, especially those involved in AI training and development, consider user data to be extremely valuable, akin to a gold mine. You know how they say "The more, the merrier."

I'm sure you all know which industry benefits the most, right?

Yup, you got it, it's social media companies. Social media was made to gather as many users as possible, and to reach as many people around the world for free. Their business model was a success, maybe even too much of a success. Today, social media websites boast a staggering 5 billion users, with a remarkable 260 million new users joining in 2023 alone.
With the development and strengthening of economies in developing countries, particularly in populous regions like Asia and Africa, there will be a noticeable rise in the usage of social media and adoption of modern technology. The potential for data gathering on these continents is immense, particularly for tech companies that highly value user data.

However, with so much control and power over user data, comes a lot of greed. Can you believe that all these big organizations have been caught red-handed selling user data to everyone, including their rivals? Very surprising. Facebook, or Meta as it is now called, is infamous for selling user data to political parties across the globe, as well as to various "research/marketing" organizations. That being said, social media's new approach to business mainly involves the selling or utilization of user data to train AI. In an effort to maximize revenue, Reddit has disclosed its plans and outlined its strategy to sell user data for training AI models, to third-party organizations like

Google and OpenAI.

The internet is so sketchy with our data, so how do we keep it safe from leaks and deep-fakes?

Well, the answer is not so simple. Since AI is in its early stages, it is impossible to predict the exact form the technology will take in the next two decades.

However, there are still actions you can take to potentially minimize the level of risks:

- Do not click on website links that someone sends you, without reading the link. Stay vigilant for shady websites that pretend to be real but are actually after your information. They can look exactly same as the actual website. For instance: If someone sends you a youtube link, but the link is not youtube.com, or youtu.be, then its more than likely to be fake to get your information.

- It's risky to overshare on social media, especially now with deepfakes. Just picture this - you post tons of pics on social media, and then someone makes explicit deepfakes of you and tries to blackmail you for cash. They threaten to "leak" the deepfake to your friends if you don't pay up. This has happened so many times, but with new tech, deepfakes are getting harder to tell apart from real pics and can mess with your emotions and mental health.

- You should **NEVER** post pictures of your kids and underage people on your profile, for their physical and mental safety.

- "**Social engineering**" is another trick you need to be cautious about. It's when people trick you into revealing personal information, to try and predict your passwords, emails, card cvv number, and other sensitive information. For example: If someone online is friendly and asks for personal information like your birthday, favorite color, or pet names, they might try to use this information to guess your password or security questions and gain access to your account. So, you should always be careful when revealing information to people. Especially the one's you don't know very well.

- Revealing personal information during arguments is another tactic that hackers use. They try to trick you into arguments where you might spill sensitive and private information, while getting you all worked up, so you don't notice they're leading the conversation.

- It's the same with so many fake websites displaying ads about "winning" a free prize, it's like throwing food to a hungry fish and watch it take the bait. Things that seem too good to be true, are usually too good to be true.

- Always make sure that your location history, and location permissions, are not set to public in websites and apps. This can give people a chance to track your location or places that you frequently visit to. You can check by going to the settings of each app, and seeing the permissions. For PC's, turning off location access for your web browser should help a lot.

- Last, but not the least, **enabling 2 factor login** or authentication for your account helps immensely. You then have to enter either a OTP(one-time-password) sent to your phone or email, or have an authenticator app to verify a code on your other devices. This way, no one can login to your account even if they guess the password(for the most part).

With the rise of AI and Smart features, the need for robust security measures becomes more apparent than ever. For organizations and startups, data is like a treasure trove, but we must be vigilant as users to prevent any misuse of our personal information. Taking precautionary steps is usually the best way to avoid a lot of common scams and helps us in protecting our identity.

In a future where AI is used to generate and reproduce images and videos, the significance of our individual identity becomes increasingly crucial. The potential for your face to be manipulated in images and videos is concerning, as it can be used for blackmail purposes and to spread false information.

With OpenAI showcasing its AI capabilities, creating realistic and high quality videos just from text prompts, that is just the start. They have also developed realistic and accurate voice replication of any individual, which can be used for a lot of bad things. They ran into some regulation issues and thus this launch was delayed.
And of course, technology, just like other things, can be used for both good and bad.

This is another step to a complete self-development; where we are aware of the risks and steer our future in a direction where we can avoid as many of them.

<u>Globalization</u>

One of the most remarkable achievements of technology is it's ability to connect and globalize the entire world. Thanks to modern technology, industries, people, and resources can now seamlessly be shared, transferred, and developed. The remarkable transformation in technology from 1996-2018 is a clear reflection of the progress achieved by most countries. With the advancement in consumerism and the development of new technologies, people can now find work that matches their skills across different countries, leading to improved economies worldwide. The improvement in infrastructure development, social connectivity, and resource management has resulted in greater sophistication and productivity.

However, this trend took a huge hit when covid-19 came along. Public opinions on globalization and opening borders to it have shifted, coinciding with a technology war between the United States and China. As a consequence, both countries have imposed sanctions on each other, leading to higher costs in global technology production and trade.
Due to the significant rise in contrasting opinions and preferences, social media websites now utilize separate algorithms and curated content for each country, a change that has spread rapidly in the last 5 years. Covid may not be solely responsible, but its influence undeniably expedited these issues at an unprecedented rate. The fear of the unknown and social isolation can deeply impact our perception and thinking, often without immediate awareness.

Now let's talk about, perhaps, the most important factor in every decision we make throughout our lives. I'll give you different perspectives to think about, as well as some suggestions.

Logical vs emotional thinking

It is a well-known fact that humans are social creatures, and just like a phone has built-in chips, our brains have built-in social needs. Yet, the choice of how to use, modify, and enhance it lies in our hands. Our thoughts and emotions are in charge of our innate desires, and we have the ability to control them. Even though controlling our actions and emotions can seem difficult at times.

Like adjusting the brightness of a phone screen when we go out in the sun, we have the power to adapt our own thoughts based on the environment we find ourselves in. It's amazing how we have the ability to control both our logical and emotional thoughts while also being aware of them. Humans have demonstrated an unparalleled level of control over their actions and emotions, a trait that no other living creature has exhibited to such an extent.

A solid understanding and control of these two mental processes are instrumental in shaping the quality of our decisions and the effectiveness of our actions. If we learn to be aware of them and control them to some extent, our quality of life is improved, our relationships are strengthened, and our productivity is enhanced. Not only that, it helps in retaining our brain capacity and maintaining memory retention as we get older, because we need to use different parts of our thinking in different scenarios. Research has consistently shown that lifelong engagement in some form of work keeps the brain sharp, lowering the likelihood of dementia and other cognitive impairments. Moreover, maintaining a daily routine helps your body stay alert, which in turn helps regulate your diet and promotes a more active lifestyle.

In the workplace, we often have to prioritize logic over emotions, while in personal relationships, emotions tend to take precedence over logic. The complexity of our brain's functioning becomes evident when considering that different tasks and people require distinct parts to process, feel, and act. I mean, if you choose not to consciously develop these skills, some aspects of your life may fall behind, affecting your quality of life or what people often refer to as "peace of mind". To realize our full potential, we have to make conscious efforts.

We all have unique personalities, so our responses to situations can vary greatly. Expanding our knowledge about others and making conscious efforts to react and respond in a more positive manner is an essential part of our human growth journey.
To do that, lets first understand how logical and emotional response actually work in real life. You know, a little bit of contrast with real life examples to help you relate and understand.

Logical vs emotional contrast:

- Logical thinking relies on analyzing information and using a structured approach to come up with solutions. Emotional thinking is more complicated and unique. When we're thinking logically, our emotions get triggered by our perception and morals, and these emotions sometimes drive us to do things differently than how we think we should ideally.

- Imagine this: you're working as an executive, and you have the task to release a new AI based software that might negatively effect a large amount of jobs within your organization. You might get stuck in a dilemma, contemplating whether you should do it or not, you think about morals, it's long term impact on others, and your reputation as well.

- The getting stuck in a dilemma is what we call our emotional response. Our emotions get triggered when we think about taking actions throughout our lives. How well we manage to control over it, depends on us.(to a lot of extent)

- We can't always do things exactly like we want, sometimes we have to go against our emotions. Especially when it's something that is personal, such as keeping your job or getting a pay raise. We cannot always have control over the decisions we make, but we can learn to minimize their effect on us.

- There is a famous quote for that "you may not control all the events that happen to you, but you can decide not to be reduced by them"-Maya Angelou. It's a pretty simple statement, but when you think about it, it talks about a lot of different things that happen behind-the-scenes a.k.a in our subconscious mind.

Now that we know about it, how do we have better control over these two?

The answer is subjective and relies on your personal beliefs and emotions towards the world. While answers may differ for each individual, having a framework enables us to evaluate our own values and reconsider our approach.

So, we're going to exactly do that.

To improve our logical thinking:

- Do activities that trigger your thinking, games such as chess, sudoku, and minecraft are great starters. It could also be certain video games that force you think harder and faster, like strategy based games. Training our brain to make decisions is something we need to keep doing throughout our lives, it helps to make sure we don't get rusty in our abilities and potential.

- Whenever we're faced with a challenge or problem, always try to break it down into different parts. Analyzing information related to a problem is always crucial, as it distinguishes good decision makers from the rest. Making logical decisions comes naturally to them, so it requires less time and energy. In the same way that professional athletes must continually practice to sharpen their instincts and respond instantly to difficult situations during intense games, the same applies to other fields where quick problem-solving is crucial. We benefit from a healthy body and brain in anything and everything we do.

- Talking about practice, we all know practice makes perfect. (*Although, perfection is impossible to achieve but you get the point.*) Regardless of our skill level, we must persistently pursue the things we desire to master, throughout our lives. To prevent our brain from slowing down, it needs regular stimulation, so it's important to keep practicing, no matter how small the effort may seem. The impact of these persistent, minor efforts become evident as we get older.

- A notable characteristic that is often found in intelligent thinkers is the ability to question their assumptions, and this trait should be valued and fostered. When we're acting on something, we should always ask ourselves "stop, why am I doing this?", "Is it because I feel like it, or is it because it is the right thing to do?", "Could I be wrong?", "What are the alternative solutions and approaches?" and so on...

Now, to the hard part: Emotional thinking

Since emotions are unique to each individual, there is no definite answer to this question. Consequently, many of us may find it difficult to relate to or comprehend certain things we come across in books or online. However, like I previously stated, adopting a blank framework to organize our emotions and employing logical thinking to deconstruct it, is the right method. I want you to think for yourself, understand your emotions, and then make your own decisions in life. There is no greater source of empowerment for self-development than the ability to understand oneself and have better control over one's thoughts and emotions. Although it may seem challenging at first, with time and practice, our new approach to decision making becomes second nature.

So here are some pointers to possibly improve our emotional thinking:

- Improving our self-awareness is the first step. Realizing and understanding how we feel about something is not a skill that is easily found. There are numerous straightforward and efficient ways to monitor them, many of which may be familiar to you. Some methods to explore for self-reflection and personal growth include journaling, recording your voice to express your emotions (especially if writing is not your preferred method), practicing meditation which is a widely recognized technique, and engaging in mindfulness which is a more recent approach encompassing various concepts. When exploring these three approaches, you will discover an abundance of methods and concepts that, with practice, will enhance your skills. Under these 4 approaches, there are countless of different activities that you can mix and match. I won't tell you which method to adopt, because again, I want you to use your AI chatbot friends to read the different methods and choose the ones that work for you. This will enable you to slowly rely on yourself, whenever you're looking for solutions. You can search for their definitions, then search for things like "What are different practices in jouranling/mindfulness?", "what are different concepts in mindfulness?", and things like that.

- Challenge your thoughts with evidence: When you feel sad, frustrated, angry, or helpless, think of evidence that proves it. Many times, our emotions are driven by unfounded beliefs rather than logical reasoning. As things happen in front of us, emotions arise instantly, like a rush of adrenaline. When that happens, we first need to let out our emotions, before trying to think logically. After taking a moment to contemplate the situation, we can begin to think of evidence to back up our feelings. Take, for instance, when you experience frustration or sadness over something that transpired at your job or school. You've come to the realization that it's having a negative impact on you, so now it's important to utilize your newly developed logical thinking skills to understand why. "When did you begin to feel sad, and what were the circumstances that occurred at that time? What could have caused it?"

- Well, the answer is not always obvious. Especially when you're new to this. By consistently asking yourself these questions when something happens in your life, you'll gradually develop the habit and slowly reach the answers. These are just some questions that can get you started on your self-challenge journey.

- Developing healthy coping mechanisms is perhaps one of the most important things that we can do for a good quality of life in every aspect. We all need ways to express and manage our stress and emotions, even when we are feeling happy. Being excited can lead us to take more daring actions than we typically would. When we're sad, we might feel like being alone and wallowing in sad thoughts, maybe even listening to sad songs or treating yourself to something sweet. Being bold and enjoying solitude are both ways to cope with our emotions. These habits might have been learned subconsciously, rather than us adopting them on purpose, but they become an integral part of our lifestyle. Learning and practicing new coping mechanisms can be challenging, particularly when we have to approach it with logic instead of acting on impulse. Nevertheless, it's not impossible.

- If you're feeling stressed and need some healthy outlets, consider going to the gym, engaging in sports activities, listening to your favorite songs, or even singing along passionately to songs that resonate with you. Oh, crying is actually healthy, and helps your brain to regulate emotions, so don't let anyone stop you from crying when you feel like it.

- Once we have the ability to recognize and classify our emotions, we can then more efficiently organize our thoughts and emotions, resulting in improved decision-making and reduced mental stress. Learning to empathize with others, even at a beginner's level, is a crucial skill to develop. It is incredibly beneficial for nurturing personal and professional connections, as well as for propelling oneself forward. Since we have to live around other humans who hold emotional capacity just like us, understanding them becomes ever so important and helps us in maintaining healthy relationships.

These skills are often overlooked and not commonly taught in various parts of the world, but they are crucial. I mean sure, we can muddle through life regardless, but having increased mastery over our own thoughts doesn't sound too bad either.

Honestly, even if we just become average at these skills, it can still benefit us in advancing our careers and forming new relationships. And who knows, those relationships might even help us grow as a person. Having good relationships with our coworkers not only improves our network, but also provides support when things get tough in the work-place.
Again, we have our AI friends ChatGPT and Google Gemini just a few clicks away. Asking them any questions regarding your emotions and logic will help you get a new perspective and get your brain running up again, for when you feel stuck.

I'll also be updating and adding new content on my website, for free. These are extensions of what I've talked about in the book. The next chapter is dedicated to talking about different possible scenarios of the future!

CHAPTER EIGHT

THE FUTURE - A LEAP OF FAITH!

In this chapter I'll be talking about the potential possibilities of how the future could look like, as technology advances further. By that time, the AI revolution would have settled, and will become an integral part of our everyday life.

These are just predictions based on the current trends, I'll take full credit if they come true. Otherwise, I'll switch up my predictions and pretend I got them right.

A Connected society

Imagine a world where technology is everywhere, there is no escaping it. Even if you go into the washroom for some peace, there will be smart-toilets.

In the near future, nearly all forms of infrastructure will include embedded chips that serve multiple purposes. These devices will facilitate communication and data transfer between different components, monitor the condition of the infrastructure, and even allow relevant authorities to take control in times of emergencies, such as disasters or wars. Satellite connectivity is another form of communication that oversees a large amount of geography without physically interrupting our society(at least on earth).

As time progresses, we can expect a vast array of private and public technologies to be powered by satellite connectivity. This could mean that cars will also have the ability to connect to this network. I mean, one of the most obvious example is Tesla connected directly to starlink for features, cloud services, and even maintenance. This helps them not just to monitor but also develop future products catered towards customers more accurately, and providing new features that are more useful and effective for customers.

There's no getting away from a connected world - our phones, wearables, cars, infrastructure, and society will be in constant communication. I suspect, there is even a possibility of wireless jammers becoming more prevalent in the future, as more and more technologies rely on wireless protocols. The government knows about this risk and will take action to avoid it, so we'll have to wait and see, will evil win over good? Find out in 2035.

A sky full of stars

Imagine seeing a night sky, shining full of stars. But wait! You zoom into the sky a little with your phone's camera and you see it's a sky full of drones and satellites.

Flying gadgets, including drones and satellites, will become MUCH more prevalent in the future. Today, as of 2024, drones are under-utilized because of many complexities since the technology is far from perfect. As AI advances, hardware improves, and everything becomes connected, it will set up the perfect environment for drones and other flying gadgets to strive in. Imagine getting important mail, your online orders, food, and whatnot delivered to you instantly. Avoiding all the human created traffic on roads, it will streamline transfer of goods and services and make it much more seamless.

It's not just delivery drones however, we'll also have small drones with LED's to create images and objects in the middle of a sky. I mean we've already seen that happening but not on a global scale at large, and its pretty expensive to execute for now. However, in the future it will be a common sight to behold! Imagine seeing ads in the middle of night when you look up, or seeing fireworks-like movements in the sky to create fascinating new visuals for entertainment. A lot of possibilities will open up once the technology adoption becomes widespread, and it might as well even light up the sky.

As with anything, this will invite new regulations to make sure its not misused. Since drones could also be used for trafficking of illegal goods and communication for illegal activities... I'm not gonna get into details about that.

Connected Humans!

Well, since the infrastructure and sky will be connected, why shouldn't we be connected to them and other humans as well?
Good news for us, we'll all have the option to connect ourselves with others, literally. Body implants, bio-hacking, and wearables will become all too common in the future. Neuralink is perhaps the most well-known implant company right now, but there are a lot of startups and new companies working on these technologies. Although it will take many, many years for these technologies to become even safe enough to be put into our body, it will happen.

There are people who have successfully implanted NFC chips and used it to make payments, connect to their devices at home and even for locking/unlocking their home. For those wondering, it was in the upper layer of the skin in our hand. But, this technology rather holds more risk, as our body's immune system becomes active as soon as it detects foreign objects, not to mention the potential of materials leaking; such as the long-term result of plastic, metal, or other material's interaction by being in contact with our blood and skin. They could possible break down, or react in ways we didn't know before and since humans have unique bodies, its impossible to have a straight answer.

However, for all the risks it holds, companies are still actively investing into this technology. Even if it is not adopted on a mass scale, it can prove to very useful for medical reasons. For people with physical and neurological conditions, especially, implants can prove to be life saver. Not to mention, constant monitoring of blood for diseases, it could even become possible to detect cancer and virus/bacteria spread as early as possible and save a large amount of people from late diagnosis.

It is also predicted to be useful for memory retention, as well as for people who have brain development issues, which traditionally might have rendered them unable to perform a lot of tasks. With the implant, they can command themselves to perform tasks, that they might not have been able to otherwise due to physical or mental limitations.

It's like you'll become part robot, part human. Maybe we'll even have a secret society of superior humans in the future.

<u>Super-humans!!</u>

Since we're on the topic of connected humans, how can we forget super humans?!
If you haven't guessed it by now, super-humans can be created artificially. Thanks to advancements in technology and AI, gene-editing has become not just possible but also viable.

Gene editing open's up the potential for humans to play god and design humans as they wish, for specific purposes. In china there were two doctors arrested for performing illegal gene-editing on infants. The doctors were trying to modify genes and create children that will be immune to HIV forever, but that is just one concept. If you've seen superhero movies, you've probably seen those evil corporations performing experiments to create human-weapons with super strength, disease free, immortal even, or have some secret powers.
Well, those concepts have never been unfounded or out of nowhere. It's just now, thanks to AI, we now have some kind of technology that makes those concepts a possibility and the goal doesn't seem unrealistic at all now. Just like implants, those concepts are all fun and fancy sounding, but it can also be used to treat genetic diseases and prevent potential spread of diseases in infants with compromised immune systems. Although, this is far more complex than implants, since this is directly modifying our biology.

There is also a possibility to constantly modify humans to survive in the drastically changing future climate. Not just for weather, but we could also create humans that need less water, can tolerate extreme weather, or even have more resistance to diseases and poison, have eyes or hair that don't age as fast and retain their capacity even when we get old. When used along with implants, It could be effective in maintaining diabetes, blood sugar levels, disease detection and even slowing down the aging of organs while also making our body more adaptable to organ transplant, so our immune system doesn't outright reject the transplant. Although this might take a lot longer than the next decade.

But then again, humans have achieved the impossible in the past, and they will keep doing so for as long as humanity exists.

Self aware robots?

We all know the advancements in AI and it's related fields directly contribute in streamlining the development of intelligent robots. Although the product is still far away, but we'll eventually have robots with their own mind. They will be designed with specific personalities to perform tasks, respond to human actions and conversations instantly, just like how a real human would. Once enough time has passed after that, they will slowly start to develop their own personality as they gather more experience of the real world.

Although, there are a lot of ethical boundaries in robotics.The training data used to design personalities, especially in the case of robots, is deliberately kept vague. This has led to suspicions that robots can be programmed with numerous morally corrupt traits. Unlike humans, who possess consciousness, robots can perform immoral and unethical tasks without experiencing any remorse, as they lack the emotional and physical responses that are innate to human nature!!!

These things can help us in removing humans from physically and mentally harmful jobs such as mining, so we can focus our human resources into newer jobs that will be created as a result of AI implementation.
Robotics will also play a huge role in the military across countries. We could see a large amount of foot soldiers being replaced by enhanced robots, which could result in saving a large amount of causalities in times of war.
As well with disaster relief, places inaccessible by humans can be accessed by robots. They can sync the latest data of the situation via satellite and other connected infrastructure, and then perform tasks of saving people or

providing relief, even to put out forest fires. Robots can be designed for specific scenarios and disasters, and have a lot of flexibility in both physical and mental capacity.

The virtual world

With the introduction of Apple's vision pro, AR and VR are finally entering the mainstream market. From here on, the path only goes up up and up. And it's not just those big-ass glasses that make you stand out, but a lot of other new products that will benefit from this technology. We'll see windshields with AR, identifying, displaying, and projecting visuals to assist the driver and the AI in the car, to avoid potential accidents and even for self-diagnosis. The same could be used in other vehicles and different forms of transport. AR could also be used for surgery assistance, if they work 100% accurately. Literally anything we do in real life, can be assisted by AR as long as it works smoothly in real-time and is responsive.
Professions like construction, mining, architecture, and maintenance of large buildings will all benefit.

We could see AR being used for advertisements into different products, and companies using it for presentations and better visualization. As AR advances and becomes easier to integrate into real life, we will see a large amount of new applications of those products come up.

As for VR, some of their current biggest applications are gaming, visualization, simulators for different industries such as aviation, space, and meta-verse. As AI advances and VR technology improves, we'll see a lot more uses for it. It can be, accurately, used to visualize technical data for different branches of science, accurately visualize measurements for designing, architecture, and engineering, while many other industries and professions such as sports, music, and entertainment will benefit from large scale VR adoption as well.
It could help us advance and make more accurate cures for diseases, while also assisting in designing hardware such as chips, that are very crucial for AI to function effectively and efficiently.

AI assisting humans in designing better chips for AI's future, it's already starting...

As with other technologies, I'd say one of the potential issues with the use of VR is that our senses suddenly get overwhelmed with a completely different perception of distance, objects, and reality. It messes with our senses, and many people who used Apple vision pro for long hours reported that they needed some time to adjust back to reality, after taking them off.

Another major issue is the impact of constantly having a display right infront of our eyes. We all know screens are not healthy for our eyes, and keeping a certain distance helps in reducing eye strain, but what happens when we are strapping screens right to our eyes while also creating a tunnel vision so our eyes can only focus on the screen? Not to mention, long-term screen usage has been associated with poor blink rate, causing strain and dry eyes, which in turn can cause other issues in our vision if not taken care of.

Potential, unlimited potential

Technology is such a broad term that we can invent hundreds of new products and concepts under it. As with the unlimited potential of human brain, what we can create with this brain also carries unlimited potential. Humanity has strived and survived for thousands of years thanks to our inventions, and it will keep doing so as we go into the future. Albeit it might be very different from what we have been used to in the last 100 years. Nevertheless, something that remains static is humans constantly trying to advance and create new tools as means to achieve things that are not physically or mentally possible by an individual. Whether these inventions have a positive or negative impact is a different topic.

There is no limit to the potential of how our brain can think, and what it can think. Everyone is unique and the amount of data, perspectives and skills that are shared when different individuals work together is something very unique to humans as a species. Technology is just another medium of human collaboration to achieve the impossible.

A concluding message to all of you!

Wherever you are in life, regardless of your age, skills, and knowledge. It is never too late to start from scratch. If you've longed to learn a skill from your childhood but you still haven't, its time to do it now. If you have hobbies that can be monetized in one way or another, its time to try now! If you think you're too old to change, WRONG! Who knows, you might actually grow your audience. Social media can be a powerful tool for when you're starting out and need to increase visibility for your products and services.

Achievements are the single most impactful notion that most of us yearn for. It doesn't have to be a billion dollar idea or something very big. As long as you achieve something, that is commendable in itself, because you're not only putting your skills to use but also growing and enhancing your brain's capacity to think, feel, and solve problems. Achievening even small goals, fuels the reward system in our brain, which then makes us happier and more motivated to go further. Small achievements could even include just being able to go the gym everyday or following a strict diet, that is commendable in itself and will slowly train your brain. You know how some people say they suddenly feel happy or motivated? It's because something in their thoughts or emotions triggered a rush.

Self-development is all about learning not only about yourself but the world, functioning in such a dynamic global world requires us to learn about what's happening globally. Even if nothing else, just learning new things keeps our brain's gears running.

It could just be news, about any topic you're interested in, like tech, psychology, music, movies, latest trends, anything that interests you. It could even be watching movies and breaking down the story of it. You could take any topic of your interest and try to think of it in-depth, rather than just on the surface headlines.

BUT, NEVER STOP LEARNING!

Until Next time,

N J Sharma